THE FIRST WORD OF THE KINGDOM

(PICTURES OF REPENTANCE)

HENRY A. WASHINGTON

WASHINGTON HOUSE
PUBLISHING

The First Word Of The Kingdom
by Henry Washington

Published by WASHINGTON HOUSE PUBLISHING
Mailing Address: 3600 S. Oceanshore Blvd., #216
Flagler Beach, FL   32136

Printed in the United States of America

ISBN-13:   978-0-9794179-0-0
ISBN-10:   0-9794179-0-2

Unless otherwise indicated, Bible quotations are taken from *The King James* Version of the Bible.

Cover photograph by Diddi Washington

www.henrywashington.com

Suggested Donation: $10.99

For Franny

My constant cheerleader, editor, American mom and the greatest advocate for repentance that I know.

Contents

Introduction

During my travels to churches in the past few years I have been confronted with a shocking reality. More and more churchgoing people have little or no understanding of the necessity of true Biblical repentance. I have met many people who have come forward for prayer for all types of emotional, spiritual, and physical needs who are surprised when I share with them the need to repent of certain behaviors that are ruining their lives. Others are seeking some relief from bondage in their spiritual lives. Many people have not heard the first word that Jesus preached (Matt. 4:17): ***"Repent, for the kingdom of heaven is at hand."***

Today, it seems that many people have responded to invitations to receive salvation without any mention of the need for repentance. They are invited to receive or accept the Lord with little reference to anything that Jesus has required to enter His Kingdom. They have come in obedience to the instructions given to them. Yet, they have little conviction that they are a sinner who is alienated from the life of God.

Like people who are trying to drive their cars without any gas, people are attending church, singing, praying, and trying to generally participate in church life without having truly entered into God's Kingdom. Others may have been truly saved but have seen their spiritual lives stall some time after their initial decision. There seems to be widespread silent frustration for many people who lack reality and joy in their spiritual lives.

At this present time in the Western Church there would seem to be a new approach to sin. Many people will readily acknowledge that Jesus died for mankind's sins but there seems to be a disconnection concerning what is required to be saved from sin. Many today recommend that we simply accept the free and unconditional salvation that they claim Christ will give to anyone who asks. To hear some tell the story of Jesus, you might think that God is like a salvation vending machine, dispensing salvation upon the request of the hungry consumer. They claim that if you simply admit you are a sinner and ask God's forgiveness by reciting a 'sinner's prayer' that you will be saved from the consequences of your actions.

A troubling outgrowth from this generally accepted mode of presenting the Gospel, is a generation of churchgoers who think they are saved in their sins rather than from them (Matt. 1:21). In fact, the idea of sin as a cosmic disaster, a disruption of the whole order of creation, and a matter of grave danger has been departed from in the present Western Church. The general idea that pervades many churches is that sin is expunged by Christ's blood and we just try our best to be good people.

This pervasive point of view stands in opposition to the first imperative that Jesus presented upon the imminent arrival of the Kingdom of Heaven (Matt. 4:17). This imperative was that any who wanted to enter the Kingdom of God had to repent. The word repent conveys the idea that an individual must experience a complete change of mind concerning their relationship to God, His Kingdom, their rebellion against Him (sin), and the solution for their alienation from Him. Such a change of mind would leave no area of the life untouched. In fact, saving faith's primary act is for a person to sorrow after a godly manner. We must humbly seek God. After all, He is the only One who can grant such a change.

Jesus did not just tell men to repent at the beginning of His ministry. We see that all through His ministry on earth

He illustrated what this repentance actually looked like. Through both parable and teaching Jesus gave us **pictures of repentance** that show us what the genuine article would look like. To receive Jesus as the LORD of our life brings forgiveness for sure but the whole tone of the New Testament is that of transformation. Jesus came to bring His Kingdom into men's hearts, not just in the future but in the present. Those who are thus granted repentance are able to *"bring forth fruit"* (John 15:16; Romans 7:4). Jesus clearly taught us that it is God's plan that this fruit should remain. John the Baptist taught that such righteous fruit was essential to true godly repentance (Matt. 3:8).

This book sets forth no new or exotic doctrines. Rather, I simply present some of the instruction of Jesus, Paul, and the other New Testament writers about how it is that we are to repent. Since a profound change of mind is the first imperative given by Jesus to enter His Kingdom, it logically follows that we need to get repentance right. It is my prayer that as you examine the simple teaching of the Bible that you will find this repentance to be a joyful and liberating event. Rather than having to 'give up' things that we hold dear we will find our hearts continually liberated to do the will of God, with joy.

As God gives us a complete change of mind we find that we are set free to do the things of God that we never thought we would be able to do. Rather than being a drudge, repentance becomes the happy doorway to liberty and freedom. This freedom is not to do as we wish, which is license. His freedom is to do what Jesus has commanded us, which is liberty. We then find what Jesus has said to be true: *"If the Son therefore shall make you free, ye shall be free indeed."* (John 8:36). Come with me and let us participate in applying these 'Pictures of Repentance' so that we may enter the Kingdom of God.

Chapter 1

Repent!

The first word given to men as a response to the arrival of the Kingdom of God was *"repent, for the kingdom of heaven is at hand"* (Matt. 4:17). This is the first mention of the Kingdom of Heaven or the Kingdom of God. According to standard Scriptural interpretation techniques (hermeneutics), the first mention of a topic sets the tone for understanding the subject. Simply, because repentance is mentioned first in relation to God's Kingdom, it becomes of primary importance in relation to how we may enter into that Kingdom. It is our first commanded response. It is our first act of faith upon hearing the Gospel. Repentance is the only way that we may enter into what God has for us as servants in His Kingdom. There are a few words in the Greek text to assist us to understand the basic nature of this repentance. Jesus also uses many illustrations and stories to show the essential aspects of this repentance.

The word repent comes from the Greek word **metanoeo**. This is the central word for repentance and refers to a complete change of mind for the better as it relates to God and His rule. It will also include turning away from sin and all that leads away from the LORD. Repentance goes far beyond simple mental assent or human sentiment. It affects the whole heart and mind of the person who repents. Simply, we acknowledge and receive the truth presented in the Bible that God is always right and all of mankind is wrong. In short, all of us are sinners without exception. Further, to repent is to acknowledge a willingness to have our lives changed and our behavior amended. God does this by the means of grace that Jesus has provided for us. His sacrifice as a substitute for us upon the Cross of Calvary and the power of His resurrection, give us the power to live for Him.

It helps to understand that all of our sin comes from the wrongful government of our lives. We are born with the original sin of Adam and Eve ruling us: ***"by one man sin entered into the world, and death by sin"***. (Romans 5:12). We commit acts of sin. We are guilty of committing 'The Sin' of Lucifer. 'The Sin' refers to putting ourselves on the throne of our own hearts and claiming ownership of our own lives. When I rule my own life, I become the government; in effect the 'god'. This aligns me with Satan's kingdom. When I am so aligned, my mind is darkened and I give the devil grounds to rule my life. In such a state my life is aligned with Satan's in his rebellion against God. Thus, without Christ, we are all governed by the devil, usually without even knowing it. We have aligned the government of our lives with Satan's rule and his spirit rules us (1 Cor. 2:14; 2 Cor. 2:4).

This rebellion causes me to believe 'The Lie'. 'The Sin' is claiming government over my own life. 'The Lie' is that this self-government will bring success and satisfaction with it; that I may somehow be pleasing to God or be like God. This is what Paul is driving at in Second Thessalonians Chapter Two. A major theme of the first twelve verses is that Satan's intent is to get into God's Temple and rule. Believers are God's Temple, individually, locally, and universally. Satan's goal is to entice all believers to believe "The Lie". The devil doesn't need to possess a man to get on the throne of that man's heart. All the devil needs to give him grounds for ownership is for a man to be on the throne of his own heart. That rebellion aligns us with him. Roman 1:25 tells us that believing 'The Lie' will cause people to worship and serve ***"the creature more than the Creator"***. The exaltation of self over God started with

Satan and reproduced its results in the Garden when Eve desired to be *"as gods"* (Gen. 3:5).

When we repent we are giving up all hope of pleasing God through our own means—we relinquish all self-justification. Repentance requires that we admit that we are sinners. We are admitting that we have ruled our lives and that the resulting sin and mess is our fault. This includes forsaking any fostering of 'The Lie' which would make us think that we can produce anything in our lives that will be pleasing to God. As well, we must acknowledge 'The Sin' of ruling our lives and forsake all future claims to the right to govern our own lives. Instead, we trust in the sacrifice of Christ alone for our salvation: *"For by grace are ye saved through faith; and that not of yourselves: it is the gift of God: Not of works, lest any man should boast."* (Eph 2:8-9). We then lean upon His grace alone to be kept from sin and evil. God's grace becomes the sole means for living the Christian life because we: *"are kept by the power of God through faith unto salvation ready to be revealed in the last time."* (1 Peter 1:5).

The word translated Kingdom comes from the Greek word *basileia*. This word does not really refer to our modern understanding of a kingdom—a king and his subjects. Rather, *basileia* speaks of the right and authority of a person to rule. This explains the seeming conflict. We see no visible Kingdom of God on earth. Neither does it yet appear that God's order has been set up. In the Bible we see that this will come to pass in the future. Nevertheless, through Jesus' complete defeat of Satan on the Cross (Col. 2:14-15), Jesus has the complete authority and right to rule within any who will yield to Him as their Lord. Although His reign (Kingdom) is unseen, it progresses through an individual's life until every area is brought under His dominion. It is like yeast moving through a lump of dough or the growth of mustard from a tiny seed—it starts small and soon becomes pervasive (Matt. 13:32-33).

Jesus has invaded the present with His future coming Kingdom. Men are aligning themselves now with one of two governments: that of Satan or Jesus. All will come under the eventual rule of Christ: either in heavenly cooperation or eternal damnation. John the Baptist was making this clear when he declared that Jesus would *"baptize you with the Holy Ghost and with fire"* (Matt. 3:11). The Jewish eschatological understanding at the time of Jesus was that Israel's coming King would gather His people together and judge the enemies of His Kingdom with fiery retribution. This will occur at the return of Jesus to earth. Repentance is simply aligning one's self with the winning side in the mammoth cosmic battle between God and His rebellious creatures. The urgency of repentance must not be missed because each life is truly short in the light of eternity.

The other words used in conjunction with repentance are *strepho* or *epistrepho.* They both refer to 'turning' and are translated converted. Repentance deals mainly with the mind while conversion deals mainly with the living out of our faith. In Matt. 18:3, Jesus told the disciples: *"except ye be converted, and become as little children, ye shall not enter into the kingdom of heaven"*. This related to their outward behavior, not just their mental assent to His teaching. Jesus taught that a change of mind towards God needed to be accompanied by a change of direction that would be apparent to everyone who met them.

During his second sermon, recorded in the Third Chapter of the Acts of the Apostles, Peter tied together the change of the mind with the change in behavior. In response to the convicted cry of his audience about what their response should be to the Gospel message he stated: ***"Repent ye therefore, and be converted, that your sins may be blotted out, when the times of refreshing shall come from the presence of the Lord"*** (Acts 3:19). It is really not logical to think that one can truly change their mind toward God without a complete reversal in their life. The reality of a new and different government (God's) will always bring about changes consistent with the policies of the One governing. This is true in the worldly model and is certainly true in the eternal model brought by Jesus Christ. When Christ rules in a person's heart, His government will be easily discernable in that person's behavior.

Repentance is irrevocably tied to the forgiveness of our sins. It is clear that the popular practice of simply requesting forgiveness or making a confession is insufficient. There are a vast number of Scriptures that teach that, ***"Faith without works is dead"*** (James 2:20, 26). Only a profound change of mind is sufficient to bring about saving faith and forgiveness. The idea that God is waiting for us to 'accept' His salvation is foreign to the Scriptures. Standing in opposition to this popular modern idea, Acts 17:30-31 states that God:

> *now **commandeth** all men every where to repent. **Because** he hath appointed a day, in the which **he will judge the world in righteousness** by that man whom he hath ordained (Jesus); whereof he hath given assurance unto all men, in that he raised him form the dead*

Notice that God does not request but commands men to repent. This is consistent with an appropriate acknowledgement of God as God—He rules.

A lack of conviction concerning sin and the need to change our behavior is probably the single greatest challenge to the preaching of the Gospel in America today. In fact, if people are making 'decisions' for Christ without the conviction that they are a hell-bound sinner and an enemy of God, the question must be raised "What are people then being saved from?" It is unlikely that a person will repent if they don't really believe that they are a sinner. Such a 'decision' then becomes little more than a wish to go to heaven or a vote for Jesus. It is clear that this is not what our Father in heaven is seeking for us.

Some people would like to argue whether one would have faith first and repentance would follow or one would repent and saving faith would follow. I don't know. Today, some are teaching that believing is repentance and vice versa. Only a cursory look at the original language will show us that repentance and faith are different activities. Nevertheless, they are inextricably linked. Paul the Apostle was very clear. He stated that he taught the same thing to everyone he preached to: ***"repentance toward God, and faith toward our Lord Jesus Christ"*** (Acts 20:21). One does not have faith if they have not repented of their sins and one who has repented of their sins is showing saving faith toward God.

The confession of our sins to God is the initial action of our repentance. This fact absolutely astonishes me. God has ordained that all any man needs to do is to admit his personal bankruptcy to please God and to have faith in the work of His Son as a substitute for sin on the Cross. This is the act of faith required but here is the rub—this is the very thing we don't want to do. We think, "There must be more to do... I must have something I can bring to please God." There isn't. God did it all. He took on the form of a man, lived the perfect life, atoned for our sin on the Cross, and rose again, thus validating His message. He then offers us complete salvation freely—if we will just humble our self-righteous hearts to receive the free gift that He is holding out to us. To do this we must repent of our sin.

After they make their initial profession of faith, many people then become very caught up with the other things they must now "do for God" in some sort of gratitude or service to Him. This falls far short of Biblical repentance. When asked what was necessary to *"work the works of God"*, Jesus answered that the *"work of God"* was to believe on the One whom God had sent—that is, Jesus (John 6:28-29). The Cross ceases all human effort to be good. When we repent, God makes us good. Jesus comes to live inside of our heart. No human work will add anything because without Jesus we can do nothing (John 15:5).

We must not miss what else happens when we repent of our sin. Peter gives a pattern for us in Acts 2:38 that holds a fantastic promise for any who will come to God: *"Then Peter said unto them, Repent, and be baptized every one of you in the name of Jesus Christ for the remission of sins, and ye shall receive the gift of the Holy Ghost."* Peter told the seeking crowd that they must repent. This would lead to an act of obedience in being baptized to confess their faith. This repentance and act of faith would cause their sins to be remitted. That means that God's account of each person's sin would be wiped clean.

God does not leave the vessel empty, however. Peter promised that each person would receive the Third Person of the trinity into their inner being; the precious Holy Spirit. He went on to say that this was a promise from God. It didn't just reach to the early Church or just the Jewish believer. It didn't just reach to those whom Paul later preached to. Peter said that the Holy Spirit would be given, *"to all that are afar off, even as many as the Lord our God shall call"* (Acts 2:39). This means everyone who repents will receive the Holy Spirit into their lives. He then guides them, teaches them, convicts them, and keeps them from all evil.

The ministry of the Holy Spirit is a central truth and reality for any who would believe. All legal action brought by God's justice against us is dealt with through Christ's sacrifice. Nevertheless, this is but the preparation for the coming of the Holy Spirit to the believer. When we repent of our sin and receive Jesus as our Savior, He gives us the Holy Spirit forever (John 14:16). We must learn to hear the Holy Spirit and walk with Him. Since we receive new hearts when we repent, the Holy Spirit will lead us into all the truth of the Word of God (Eze. 36:26; John 16:13). All the power of God is loosed into us as the Holy Spirit penetrates every area of our lives.

The test of Romans 10:9-10 is often given as the ultimate proof that an individual is saved:

> *That if thou shalt confess with thy mouth the Lord Jesus, and shalt believe in thine heart that God hath raised him from the dead, thou shalt be saved. For with the heart man believeth unto righteousness; and with the mouth confession is made unto salvation.*

Yet, confession and heart faith cannot be separated from the command to repent. To separate the confession of Jesus as Lord and heart-faith in Him from repentance is to meddle with Paul's clear teaching. One who has truly repented will most gladly let their entire sphere of influence know that they belong to Jesus. Their whole hope will rest in their faith in Jesus' resurrection. This can only come into being through a complete change of mind about who God is and what his claims are upon our lives.

This is evidently how Paul saw the Gospel when he was called upon to testify before King Agrippa. He told the king what he had been preaching as a result of his Damasus Road call in Acts 26:20:

But shewed first unto them of Damascus, and at Jerusalem, and throughout all the coasts of Judaea, and then to the Gentiles, that they should <u>repent and turn to God</u>, and <u>do works meet for repentance</u>.

Clearly Paul saw repentance as the first step toward entering the Kingdom of God, so it remained the central thrust of his Gospel presentation. The works of the believer's life become the greatest evidence that they have repented.

It is clear that repentance is tied to all actions of man and God at the point of salvation and going forward. Any person who repents will be converted, sanctified, justified, and glorified. The repentant soul will believe on Christ and confess Him as their Lord. They will be filled with the Holy Spirit and walk out their salvation through converted behavior. Truly, repent is the first word of the Kingdom. When Jesus comes to set up His rule in a person it will become apparent that the Kingdom of God has come near.

Chapter 2
Sort Of Sorry

In the last thirty years there has been a huge growth of what are now commonly called Twelve-Step programs. These programs use twelve steps that assist a person who is fed up with being addicted to alcohol, drugs, sex, food, and so on, to overcome their addiction. Many of the steps used have been taken right out of the Bible. They are essential steps for overcoming any sin. Such actions as admitting we have a problem or declaring that we are helpless against what enslaves us and must have God's help are very Biblical. Often, Twelve-Step groups provide much more support and honesty than can be found in the institutional church. I know many people who have received help from such groups.

The fatal flaw of the Twelve-Step program is the narrowness of the focus. Behaviorally speaking, such a program is very powerful because the individual participating is able to focus on changing an individual behavior with God's help. However, Biblically speaking, such a program becomes an example of what Paul the Apostle is speaking about when he was telling the Corinthians about *"the sorrow of the world"* (2 Cor.7:10).

The word translated *"world"* is the Greek word *kosmos*. This refers to the whole society of ungodly mankind on the earth with all of its diverse systems and governments. Thus, worldly sorrow is what we find reflected in the present, temporary system. It is reflected in all religion, human law, economics, and social morality upon the earth. While a Twelve-Step program may bring about profound change within a narrow range of behavior it falls far short of making a person whole or truly availing to

23

bring a person to a life-transforming encounter with the living God.

The sorrow of this world is the kind felt by many alcoholics. The alcoholic finally 'hits bottom' when they realize that they are addicted to alcohol. They come to understand that they can't quit anytime they want. It becomes clear that their human relationships are threatened. A husband or wife may be threatening to leave. Children may be alienated and upset. It may have become increasingly difficult to hold a job or to perform as well as they once had. They are sick and tired of being sick and tired. This causes them to 'change their mind' about drinking and resolve to finally quit. In the world system, this kind of 'reaching the end of your rope' can be very effective in bringing a person to final and lasting change in a certain area of life—in this case alcoholism.

What we are finding more and more prevalent today within the Church is what we might call partial conversions or partial repentances. Many who attend churches may speak of certain 'problems' that made them call on God. Some people testify of a profound change in one area of their life with little evident change in the rest of their life. Other 'converts' never had any concern for their sinful state at all but responded to some sort of inclusive invitation. The common thread for such professors of religious is a profound lack of conviction concerning behaviors the Bible clearly states are evil and sinful. When this type of religious person is told that their offending behavior is wrong they either disagree, saying that they don't see things that way or they become offended and defiantly tell you that, "you have no right to judge".

Often, what such a professor of religion has been offered is 'free salvation' that only hinges upon a wing and a prayer. Many today are told that all that is required for them to be 'saved' is that they 'accept' the Lord. Thus, they come with little or no conviction of sin. Others have no remorse for the evil they have done to God. There have no intention of changing their mind about those things that God's Word states are evil. They are told that if they pray the 'sinner's prayer', God will save them. Because such events often lack the conviction of the Holy Spirit, those people who are participating are doing little more than voting to go to heaven. Those praying without any real conviction do not see themselves as exceedingly sinful (Romans 7:12-14).

The sorrow of the present world is more concerned with individual sins than the indwelling nature of sin. This kind of sorrow is more concerned about the consequences of evil behavior in the 'here and now' than it is on an eternal perspective. It focuses more upon the damage done to people than the damage done to the living God. The desire of the sorrow of this world is to mitigate damage and minimize the consequences in the here and now rather than to bring transformation that will propel a person to an eternal home with their heavenly Father. Worldly sorrow seeks to renovate the soul of an individual—to fix it up for heaven rather than to allow God to transform it into a *"habitation of God through the Spirit"* (Eph. 2:22). The sorrow of this world uses the means of man to fix an individual up—it is based on the efforts of a human in the same way that Cain tried to worship God 'in his own way'.

This worldly sorrow falls short of what God requires for salvation. Most criminals have it. They are very sorry. Some feel actual remorse that proceeds from a guilty conscience. Some feel sorry that they have to bear the consequences of their actions. Others are just sorry that they were caught. They would be out doing what they pleased to this very moment if they had not been arrested.

The Bible gives some very clear examples of worldly sorrow so that we may contrast them with the sorrow that leads a person to true repentance.

Esau is a case in point. He was the elder in the family and should have received the blessing of God that was his through his birthright. Unfortunately for Esau, he had little respect for the spiritual benefits that he would receive through his birthright. The Bible tells us that he was a profane person because he placed no value on his inheritance and sold it for a meal (Gen. 25:29-34; Heb. 12:15-17). This was a matter of great consternation to God. Because of this action and the distain for holy things that was manifested by Esau, the Lord rejected him from being the one to father the descendants of Abraham who would bring forth the Messiah. In this story we see the initiative of God in choosing men according to the state of their hearts rather than the state of their status in this world. The eldest should have obtained the birthright by natural ascension but God's call transcended the natural order to award it to the individual with the right heart... Jacob.

What we do see is that Esau lived to regret his actions. The Writer of Hebrews tells us that he later sought his birthright *"with tears"* (Heb. 12:17). Esau didn't find real repentance because he never had any respect for the blessing that God would have given him. He did, however, hate the results. He found himself on the outside of the promises of God. What might have been his was given to another and that was bitter enough to bring him to tears. These were tears of sorrow, not for his offense or of repentance, but bitter tears of disappointment over the result.

Judas is another interesting case. There is little indication that Judas was going to betray Jesus in the Gospel stories except for the comments of the writers of the

Gospels. With twenty-twenty hindsight they commented that Judas would betray Jesus. There is no indication that anyone saw Jesus' betrayal coming, except for Jesus (John 6:70-71). Judas was with the others in their ministry. He was sent out by Jesus with the twelve, two by two. He preached the Gospel, healed the sick, and cast out devils in the name of Jesus, just as the others did. He lived in the presence of Jesus for over three years and heard His teaching over and over again. He was a partner with the twelve in every area of ministry.

Many of the movies that portray the life of Jesus try to give some sort of explanation of Judas' behavior. There have been sympathetic portrayals of Judas as a misguided revolutionary or a well-meaning but deceived person. The Apostle John gives us a clearer clue to Judas' behavior. Judas complained because of what he viewed as a waste of money when Jesus was anointed with costly ointment by Mary. John tells us that his motivation was greed because he was a thief and carried the money bag (John 12:4-6). There was no nobility in his actions, just avarice and, perhaps, resentment.

Judas was following Jesus but his heart was unchanged. He seemed to be part of the group but he allowed his inner urges toward evil to rule him. There was a sin problem in his life long before he sold Jesus out. Whatever his reasoning, it seems clear that Judas simply sold Jesus out for money (Matt. 26:15). Judas was a rat. He was a rat because he wanted what he wanted, period. The Bible tells us that the devil entered Judas. Nevertheless, Judas had prepared a warm place in his heart for the devil to enter (John 13:2, 26-27).

The Bible records that Judas *"repented himself"* (Matt. 27:3). The word used in the Greek is a different word than what is usually translated 'repent'. It is used to speak of a change of a person's mind about a certain decision, not to change your whole mind towards God about sin. This is apparent because of the results of Judas' worldly repentance. Peter repented of his betrayal of Jesus, wept bitterly over it, and was restored. Judas tried to give the money back, bewailed his situation, and committed suicide. His was not a saving repentance but a worldly response to his sin. It is interesting that Jesus had prayed for Peter's restoration while there is no record of any such prayer for Judas because he was the *"son of perdition"* (Luke 22:32; John 17:12).

Cain was the prototypical unrepentant man. He blazed a trail that all unrepentant men follow. It is clear that Cain and Abel had learned the appropriate way to sacrifice to God to atone for their sins. They were to sacrifice with faith toward the coming *"seed of the woman"* (Gen. 3:15). Many commentators say that God rejected Cain's sacrifice because it was not a blood sacrifice. Although this may be true, the real problem was Cain's attitude. Cain's wrong attitude is what God spoke to (Gen. 4:7). He explained to Cain that his sinful attitude was the problem—it was like a wild beast that was crouching at the door of his spiritual house, ready to pounce. Cain's only hope was to rule over his sin and the only way to win over sin is to repent of it toward God. Cain did not. He wanted to worship but he wanted to do so in his 'own way'.

It appears that Cain and Abel were able to communicate with God in a pretty direct way. God was available to them and would speak to them. Although Cain enjoyed the privilege of an opportunity of such fellowship, he chose to rage against God's rule in his life. Obviously, he couldn't do anything to God. He chose to get angry with his own brother who had showed him up with his 'goody-two-shoes' attitude. That is why Cain committed the first murder. He chose to do so with his head up. He knew it was evil and did it anyway. He cut himself off from God.

God pronounced a curse upon Cain. The thing he loved so much, agriculture, was not going to work for him anymore (Gen. 4:12). God struck at Cain's idol. His pronouncement was really about mercy. If Cain could get over his earth-loving attitude he might be restored to a proper place of forgiveness and the worship of God. Instead, Cain complained that God's sentence was too much for him to bear (Gen 4:14). Rather than repent and plead for restoration, Cain was only sorry his actions had consequences. He superimposed his own values onto mankind, expressing a fear that he would be murdered. It was hard for Cain to imagine that everyone wasn't going to behave just like him.

The characteristic that clearly comes through is how hard Cain's heart was. He started out by worshipping God in his own way. He then was angry that this attitude was completely unacceptable to God. He acted out his rage on his brother. When found out, Cain showed no remorse. Cain was only worried about his own life in the 'here and now'. He took a wife and started to raise up a line of descendants. The record is clear that he taught his children an attitude of rebellion and hardness. Lamech, Cain's great, great grandson, sang a song about his murderous attitude and career which, apparently, eclipsed Cain's (Gen. 4:18-24). This attitude fomented a pervasive attitude of rebellion on the earth that was to have deadly consequences and require God to flood the earth.

The Apostle Paul understood the need to seek the repentance that God grants. He knew that any human substitute or effort would resemble the attitude of Cain, Judas, or Esau, as well as any number of other Biblical examples. Worldly sorrow over our sin may bring change but it will never produce the results that God desires.

Worldly sorrow always depends on the initiative and effort of man rather than the mercy and grace of God. Salvation is really about what God does, not what men do to TRY to please God in THEIR OWN WAY. God requires a, *"broken and contrite spirit"* (Psalm 34:18; 51:17) in those that would draw near to Him.

This is why Paul wrote to the Corinthians that: *"the sorrow of the world worketh death"* (2 Cor. 7:10). If we repent after the manner prescribed by this world our motives will be all wrong. We will pick and choose what we feel is needed rather than admitting our whole way of thinking has been wrong. It then becomes a partial change of mind. We will feel that some sins must go for our own good but if other sins do not bother us we will not give them over to the Lord. The only way to enter God's Kingdom is to come completely in His way with humility. Anything else will be eternally deadly.

Chapter 3
Godly Sorrow

The Church at Corinth had endured some sort of great upheaval. Paul the Apostle had sent a letter of correction before the writing of what we call Second Corinthians. He had corrected some individual in the church for doing some sort of evil. In Second Corinthians he had to deal with some other problems in the church but he did take the time to commend them for their reaction to his correction. In fact, Paul told them to allow the repentant soul back into the church fellowship. He contrasted two reactions to the revelation of sin—godly sorrow and the sorrow of this world. He was pleased that the Corinthians had sorrowed after a godly manner (2 Cor. 7:8-12).

The people in the Corinthian Church had been Christians for many years. They had been walking a long and winding road in the process of sanctification—growing more and more similar to Christ by the work of the Holy Spirit in them. The Holy Spirit makes the Word of God come to life within all who believe. This process was assisted by Paul, who had taught and instructed the Corinthians in the Word. He also had the God-given courage to continue to correct the Corinthians (whom he had led to Christ) in spite of the fact that they became quite angry and rebellious about his correction. In fact, they wanted to replace him with other leaders (2 Cor. 10-12).

One aspect of the process of sanctification is the occasional realization that we are doing something that is wrong or associating with others in a way that calls for us to repent. As with our original life-changing repentance toward God, we sorrow towards Him and are granted a change of mind and attitude concerning our sin. This repentance enables us to leave our sin behind. Although we may fall down many times before finally overcoming a particular sin, our mind towards it will always be the same. We will not want to practice sin and will be convicted that it is in opposition to our Father and His reign. True repentance always changes a person's mind in a permanent way. This change is then followed by a change in lifestyle that reflects the true desires of the changed heart.

In their quest to be liberal-minded and 'loving' the Corinthians had 'tolerated' an individual who was having sex with his step-mother (1 Cor. 5:1-2). Whether this is the person who had repented and was being spoken of in Second Corinthians or it was another, it is clear that the Corinthian Church had a wrong idea about what love was. Whatever correction Paul had given them concerning the sin in their midst had struck them to the heart. They were very willing to make whatever changes were needed to be right in the sight of God.

Paul called their reaction *"godly sorrow"* which had worked true repentance in their hearts (2 Cor. 7:9-10). Paul then outlined the characteristics that such godly sorrow would produce (2 Cor. 7:11):

> *For behold this selfsame thing, that ye sorrowed after a godly sort, what carefulness it wrought in you, yea, what clearing of yourselves, yea, what indignation, yea, what fear, yea, what vehement desire, yea, what zeal, yea, what revenge! In all things ye have approved yourselves to be clear in this matter.*

We may use these characteristics to discern the quality of repentance in our own lives.

The term *"ye sorrowed"* is better rendered *"you were made sorry"*. Once the Corinthians had realized their

32

wrong-doing in their toleration of open sin in their fellowship, they were deeply moved with conviction over their culpability with the offending party. They became deeply, sincerely, and profoundly sad that they had done the wrong thing. Paul saw their sorrow as a primary motivator for a change of mind towards God.

So much is done in our day to make the Gospel palatable to the general public. Many believers feel it is offensive that a Gospel presentation should make an unbeliever uncomfortable, let alone sorry. In contrast, Paul understood the absolute necessity for a person to see their offense as it related to God and sorrow over it. Paul preached *"repentance toward God and faith toward our Lord Jesus Christ"* (Acts 20:21). It is essential that we understand that our sin is the very thing that separates us from God. Jesus was manifested to take away our sins and when we walk with Him he causes us to depart from our sin (1 John 3:5-6). Jesus did not just go to the Cross with the purpose of atoning for our sin but with the desire that we would be made free from the power of sin. In the light of God's attitude toward sin it is highly appropriate that one would feel deep sorrow over all that offends the LORD.

The Prophet Ezekiel had this idea as a recurrent theme. Jehovah was promising to forgive and purify God's people (Eze. 36:29-33; 20:40-44; 16:61). God stated through the prophet that people who were redeemed from sin would remember their own evil ways and *"lothe (sic) yourselves in your own sight for your iniquities and for your abominations"* (Eze. 36:31). This is not a matter of continual self-condemnation but a true change of heart. One who sorrows in a godly way will take no pride or satisfaction in their past sin career but will hate even the memory of it. They will not testify of their extensively evil sin career but of the good things that God has done for them since they have been saved.

The first characteristic of godly sorrow is translated *"carefulness"* in the KJV. In other places it is translated diligence. It may be best rendered *"earnest care"*. Those who come under Father's conviction care about the fact that they have done wrong. To the outside observer, their reaction may seem a little overboard since the world recommends moderation in all expression of sorrow over sin. The idea of carefulness here is that their hearts were excited with conviction that motivated them to repent. This influenced the offending individual to act in response to conviction of wrong-doing.

Next, the term *"clearing of yourselves"* is used. Whatever the offense was that Paul was speaking of, the Corinthians wanted to remove themselves from any complicity with it. This is very important. Paul had earlier exhorted the Corinthians to *"come out from among"* the idolaters of Corinth (2 Cor. 6:17). If we associate and sympathize with the sinful lives of those who are determined to do evil, it will always eventually lead to our downfall. The Corinthians wanted to disassociate them-selves from the evil that had been done in their midst.

In Jude we are exhorted to hate *"even the garment spotted by the flesh"* (Jude 23). The idea is the lingering smell that might get upon a person sitting around a campfire. Those led to Christ through the fear of the Lord don't want the smell of the smoke of their sin to linger around them any longer. Truly repentant people have had enough of their sin career.

The word *"indignation"* might be better rendered *"dis-pleased"*. The Corinthian believers abhorred and detested the wrongdoing that had taken place in their midst. We might say they were 'grossed out'. When God commended

Job to Satan, He gave a simple description of the virtues that pleased Him. Job *"feareth* (reverenced) *God and escheweth evil"* (Job 1:8, 2:3). Escheweth is obviously an archaic word. The word is best translated: "turn off or turn away from something". In other words, we are to be totally turned off by what offends God. It is not sufficient to say that we love the Lord. Most who profess to know Jesus will quickly affirm they love Him. What really delights Jesus is when we align our hearts with Him in hating evil.

One of the main characteristics of God's eternal city is that nothing evil will dwell there because, above all, God is holy and that which defiles cannot dwell with Him (Rev. 21:27). Today, many who profess to love the Lord also love all sorts of things that God has said that He hates. Job hated what God hated. He was so concerned to please God that he offered sacrifices for His children after they had celebrated their birthday feasts just in case they had done anything to offend the Lord (Job 1:4-5).

Next, we see that godly sorrow produced *"fear"* in the Corinthian believers. Jesus was very clear that we should not be afraid of what men could do to us. He was also clear that we need to fear God. God's judgment will determine our eternal destiny (Matt. 10:28). Many err in this area. They are persuaded that you don't have to fear a loving God. Scripture does not support this view of love. God is love but He is just. Although a believer does not live his life with terror he has become aware of the *"terror of the Lord"* (2 Cor. 5:11).

The Bible states that: *"The fear of the LORD is the beginning of wisdom"* (Ps. 111:10; Prov. 9:10). It is important to start at the beginning. There are many other benefits of fearing the Lord. These benefits include justice (2 Chron. 19:7), personal purity (Psalm 19:9), a good life (Psalm 34:11ff), true knowledge (Prov. 1:7), a hatred for evil (Prov. 8:13), a longer life (Prov. 10:27), strong confidence (Prov. 14:26), riches and honor (Prov. 22:4), the abiding presence of the Spirit of God (Isaiah 11:2-3), and genuine Christian fellowship (Acts 9:31), just to name a few. True repentance will always be marked by reverential awe and the fear of the Lord.

The term *"vehement desire"* might be modernized to read *"earnest desire or longing"*. What were the Corinthian believers longing for? In this context, with so many other positive characteristics being listed, it is likely that Paul is referring to their longing for God. Godly sorrow brings a realization that a person has been out of fellowship with God, in His will. As the heart turns, there is a hunger to be restored and live in the will of God again. Jesus has given a precious promise to every person who *"hungers and thirsts"* after His righteousness: *"they will be filled"* (Matt. 5:6). I have found that there have been many times when I haven't had a strong desire to seek the Lord or do His will. At that time I pray, "Lord, fill me with a hunger and thirst for You and Your presence". God is so faithful because He is always ready to answer such requests.

"Zeal" (ardor) is something that is in short supply today within the North American Church. Yet, Jesus was zealous. It seems that we want to moderate the zealous person because it is so culturally inappropriate to appear to be a 'religious fanatic'. Zeal is very popular in our secular society. World-wide it is thought appropriate to express opulent expression of support and adoration for sporting teams and personalities. Actors, musicians, authors, and even occasionally, political leaders have followings of ardent admirers. Almost everything is acceptable, including illegal deeds that will show that a person is an enthusiastic fan. It is interesting that the word fan traces its roots to the word 'fanatic'.

People **will** have zeal, for we all were built to burn with fiery desire for God. Those who align themselves with God's Kingdom will become 'fans' of Jesus. In fact, those who have truly repented become very single-minded concerning the sole importance of knowing and living for Jesus. There was a woman who washed Jesus' feet with her hair in the middle of a dinner engagement (Luke 7:36-48). This was completely over the top and offended the religious people who saw it. After all, the woman was a well known sinner in that part of the city. Jesus used the simple illustration that those who are forgiven a large debt will be more appreciative than those who are forgiven a small one. It is often the case that people who have large sin careers will be the most ardent and faithful followers of Jesus—simply because of gratitude.

The Authorized Version's translation of *ekdikesis* as *"revenge"* is probably not appropriate in this context. It would not be consistent with Christian charity to exact revenge. Rather, the work can be translated *"to do justice for all parties"*. The point is, after they sorrowed over their sins, they made things right. In the church fellowship, with both the offending party and the injured party, their godly sorrow had motivated them to make things right.

Repentance will cause positive change. Repentance will not just change the mind of a person but bring a corresponding change in behavior. If some harm has been done, the repentant person will, as much as possible, make restitution, offer an apology, and ask for forgiveness. They will do whatever else may be called for. They will throw aside their concern for their reputation or their own comfort and do what is right.

It is clear that the professing church has been quite slack in recommending restitution to new converts or repentant congregants. The story of Zacchaeus shows the power of restitution in repentance (Luke 19:1-10). When Zacchaeus told Jesus that he was going to make restitution according to the Law of God, Jesus told him, *"this day is salvation come to this house"*. It would not have been very impressive to say he was sorry for cheating people and stop there. True godly repentance demanded that he made things right with those he had misused.

As a teenager I believe I was probably well known for borrowing little bits of money from all sorts of people. I was not nearly as diligent in repaying the debt. When I had first come to Jesus, I came under a great conviction that I should pay all of those little debts off. I had to sit down and figure out everyone I could think of that I owed money to and make a list. I then had to seek each one out and repay my debts. These people would never have listened to me if I just told them I had become a Christian but some did when I repaid my debt to them.

Finally, Paul said that they had united together with a pure response in the matter at hand. The word *"clear"* is better rendered *"pure or reverential"*. Paul was affirming that their godly sorrow and ensuing repentance was evident and appropriate. This verse gives us the characteristics of the kind of repentance that godly sorrow will produce. It is clear that many Evangelicals and Full-Gospel Churches are afraid to recommend such extremes but the Scripture does. It seems that any person who really becomes deeply convicted of their sin and their need will come through to a profound conversion and change in their life—if they will repent. By the same token, it is becoming more and more clear that those who undergo little conviction or sorrow for their sin will exhibit little evidence of a change in their life.

This is why Paul contended so earnestly for godly sorrow. Paul wrote many sin-lists in his letters (Romans 1:18ff; Gal. 5:17-26; Eph. 4: 22-32; Col. 3:5-9). Although

Paul's lists were not exhaustive, he wrote them because he knew that sin is the damnable deadly spiritual disease that put Jesus on the Cross. He wanted all who heard him to depart from all iniquity and sin. There is little doubt that Paul had seen plenty of the sorrow of the **kosmos** (the world system) in his ministry. He had seen the transformation that the Spirit of God brought to bear in working conviction and godly sorrow in individuals. That is why Paul was adamant about godly sorrow.

Even though this sorrow will cause grief and upheaval in an individual's life it will also get results. The same has been seen in history. In times of spiritual awakening, revival has always been accompanied by a great conviction of and sorrow over sin. Where such godly sorrow has been present, the entire spiritual landscape of a region or a country has been transformed. The Gospel must be presented in the same way today if we hope to have the same results. The clear and anointed preaching of *"repentance toward God and faith toward our Lord Jesus Christ"* will still bring the Biblical result of transformation (Acts 20:21; Heb. 6:1).

Finally, we see Jesus profoundly illustrating true godly sorrow in His story of the Prodigal Son. Though often neglected, we need to pay attention to what the wayward boy rehearsed before he went to his father (Luke 15:17-19):

And when he came to himself, he said, How many hired servants of my father's have bread enough and to spare, and I perish with hunger! <u>*I will arise and go to my father*</u>*, and will say unto him, Father,* <u>*I have sinned against heaven*</u>*, and* <u>*before thee*</u>*, And am* <u>*no more worthy to be called thy son*</u>*: make me as* <u>*one of thy hired servants*</u>*.*

Don't miss the craftsmanship of Jesus in the story. Although we see that the father accepted him when he returned (v. 20), Jesus is clearly showing us the Prodigal's state of mind. First and foremost he had sinned against God. Then he had sinned against his own father. Finally, he acknowledged that he was not worthy to be forgiven or even to be a son. He would take the place of a servant.

This is very poignant and yet how many people come to God as if they deserve to be forgiven? No one deserves God's mercy. God extends His mercy because He **is** love. So many people are sitting in church pews that still need to come to themselves and see their need for godly sorrow. Let us take every sin to the Cross of Jesus for it is clear that our God will abundantly pardon. As we experience true sorrow over our sin we will also experience a profound change of mind—repentance.

Chapter 4
Settle Out Of Court

The concept of plea-bargaining to settle criminal charges has become pretty well known today because many people have seen it done on crime shows on television. We see the District Attorney attempting to avoid the time and expense of prosecution by offering a reduced sentence for crimes committed. If the criminal believes what is being offered is the best they can do, and if they are truly guilty of the crime, they may take the deal to reduce the consequences of their actions.

In the arena of civil law, American society has become very litigious. People are liable to sue over just about any contentious issue. Again, depending on the merits of any particular case and the expense of fighting it, people may choose to seek a settlement that would satisfy the litigant and be suitable to the person being sued. There may be a great deal of negotiation because both sides may have valid claims that have to be considered. It is often much more economical to settle a valid case than to fight it out to the bitter end.

In the Sermon on the Mount, Jesus started to lay out how people who are part of God's Kingdom will behave. Rather than just stressing external behavior, every beatitude and principle that Jesus taught would proceed out of a person's heart. It appears that this block of teaching gives us a thumb-nail sketch of what a Kingdom person will behave like. It is clear that this is what Christ expects His followers to be like because he framed his teaching within the context of a person entering the Kingdom of Heaven. In the Gospel of John we see that Jesus taught that a transformed heart was the only way to enter the Kingdom of Heaven (John 3:16). He would later die on the Cross to impart a new life that would enable men to obey him: *"thou shalt call his name JESUS: for he shall save his people from their sins"* (Matt. 1:21; Roman 2:26, 8:1-4). He doesn't save us in our sins but from them.

Many writers tend to idealize the teaching that Jesus brought forth. They teach that his teachings are like goals for human behavior that we must strive to obey. Much of what Jesus was teaching was further exposition on God's law. Some people believe that Jesus was simply bringing a higher 'standard' for human behavior. We now understand that the purpose of the Cross was to bring a completely new heart: *"A new heart also will I give you, and a new spirit will I put within you: and I will take away the stony heart out of your flesh, and I will give you an heart of flesh"* (Eze. 11:19; 36:25-27). Just a summary reading of the rest of the New Testament will make it clear that setting a standard was not the primary purpose of Jesus' teaching. This is because no human effort can produce the level of moral behavior that God requires. God's own salvation produces within the regenerated person the power to live as a Kingdom person.

Jesus taught that: *"except your righteousness shall exceed the righteousness of the scribes and Pharisees, ye shall in no case enter the kingdom of heaven"* (Matt. 5:20). The Pharisees were the teachers whose teaching was most closely aligned with Jesus as far as doctrine went. They treated sin like an infection and had created over six hundred extra rules that they felt, if obeyed, would create a fence of defense from breaking God's law. Many of them were very earnest and sincere. Others were hypocrites because they were just pretending that they were good. They had no way to deal with their inner evil urges and yet pretended that they did not have such urges.

So we see that the ***"Righteousness of the... Pharisees"*** was the external righteousness of human effort. There was a certain logic that went along with this view. If you were very externally religious, belonged to the right religious sect, and had the appropriate world-view (doctrine), the Pharisees would regard you as righteous. Conversely, if you broke their rules, you were poor, or you were ill, there was no doubt that these circumstances were evidence of God's displeasure and judgment on the evil in your life. Central was the comparison of one person with another in human judgment. The Pharisee was assured that God was pleased with him because he behaved well. In other words, they tried their best.

Jesus' comment that his audience's righteousness must exceed that of the Pharisees must have greatly astonished them. It is doubtful that they could have really understood what Jesus meant because they were so immersed in an atmosphere of religious self-effort. Jesus was describing a remarkably virtuous son of the Kingdom who would be humble, pure, and full of spiritual fruit. This child of the Kingdom would be so attractive that they would make people thirst for the life of God. They would spread God's light wherever they went (Matt 5:14-16). The son of the Kingdom would have no undue anger or hatred (Matt. 5:22). They would be so concerned about their fellow man that they wouldn't even try to worship if their human relationships were not in order (Matt. 5:23-24).

Any honest soul who heard Jesus then or who today reads the first twenty-four verses of Chapter Five of Matthew should be undone. Jesus inserts a curious parable after this initial block of teaching (Matt. 5:25-26). The context of this parable is peace with your brother. In Luke 12:58-59 the same parable is used but the context is completely different: loving God supremely, even above family ties, and properly discerning the signs of the times in relation to Messiah. Jesus then warns His audience:

When thou goest with thine adversary to the magistrate, as thou art in the way, give diligence that thou mayest be delivered from him; lest he hale thee to the judge, and the judge deliver thee to the officer, and the officer cast thee into prison. I tell thee, thou shalt not depart thence, till thou hast paid the very last mite.

This leads me to believe that we are to apply this parable to our relationship with God. It is not just as an illustration of being at peace with our fellow men.

In the light of the impossibility of making our hearts conform to the teaching of the Sermon on the Mount, Jesus recommended that we settle out of court with our heavenly Father. This is our first picture of repentance. Jesus is making it clear that we need to properly assess our righteousness in the light of God's righteousness. What honest person will contend that they have been the person Jesus describes in Matthew, Chapters Five to Seven? Yet Jesus asserts that this is just the kind of person who will enter God's Kingdom.

Internal honesty will lead to a profound awareness of sin and a sincere admission of guilt. One cannot truly repent of their sin until they realize the magnitude of the penalty due. Think of it. In the story, God is our adversary. We have wronged Him. He has a case against us. We have no defense. God has no fault or wrong in relation to any human being. Every human being has wronged God, *"for all have sinned and come short of the glory of God"* (Romans 3:23). Our heavenly Father needs no lawyer. He will prosecute the case Himself and His presentation of the facts will undo the most self-righteous individual.

Further, God is the judge in the story. He is the Creator of all. He upholds all of creation. He has infinite wisdom, knowledge, power, and authority. He has already issued a warrant for our arrest (Eph. 2:15; Col. 1:20-22, 2:13-15) and it is only His mercy that keeps Him from judging us immediately. He has all the evidence He needs and there is no way that He can make a mistake or look the other way, "Just this once". He will find us guilty and give us the full penalty that His law demands.

Jesus goes on to state that the punishment will fit the crime. God is in charge of the jail officer (angels) and the jail (hell). If any person foolishly insists upon going to court with God they will not get off easy. They will not get out of jail until they have paid the full price for their crimes. The price of our crimes against our Father is eternal separation from God and punishment in hell. This means that the price for our sin could never be paid by any human means.

True repentance is always characterized by an **honest assessment** of the magnitude of our crimes against God. If we will but meet Christ's terms of total surrender and true repentance from our sin, we will escape the judgment that is due to us. A person cannot truly repent until they see the magnitude of their situation. This is what Jesus is trying to illustrate through this little parable.

The attitude of any earnest soul must be to forsake any efforts and righteousness of their own for their salvation. A correct assessment of our case before God will bring us to the conclusion that we don't have a leg to stand on. Our only hope is the character of the Judge. Our Judge is just and cannot just let us off. He has provided the payment for our crimes through Jesus, if we will but avail ourselves of

His mercy. Such a realization will bring us to the place of abject humility because the very Person who is going to judge us is our only hope for acquittal.

This reminds me of an illustrative story of two very close friends who went to the same university. One studied law and, over time, became a superior court judge. After the other friend left school, he used his education to advance him in a life of white-collar crime. One day, our criminal friend was caught. He eventually appeared before his old friend, the judge. To be just and fair, the judge had to find his old friend guilty and assess a hefty fine. The criminal had no means to pay and would have to go to jail to pay the penalty. Upon hearing this, the judge left the courtroom, took off his robe, went to the cashier, and paid the fine for his friend. He had to judge his friend but he also paid the price of his crimes.

In a much greater way, our heavenly Father has paid the penalty for our sins through the sacrifice of his own precious Son. His requirement for us to receive the forgiveness of our sins is to humbly take full responsibility for our actions, to change our minds toward God, and to confess our sins to Him. We also must have faith towards His son Jesus as a sacrifice who fully atoned for the price of our sin on the Cross (Romans 5:10, 11).

The person who tries to meet God on any other terms will find themselves involved in a hopeless court case before God. Who can stand and proclaim themselves 'not guilty' in His court of law (Isaiah 59:12; Psalm 24:3,4; 76:7; 130:3)? Who will be able to persuade the King of the universe that they have been perfect in all of their behavior, attitudes, and motives? We know the answer: no one.

An inadequate repentance will eventually bring about a feeling of self-righteousness. Many who name the name of Christ have a sense of superiority about them. They think that they are somehow good, better than their fellow man. There comes to their life a sense of superiority in their mind. They exalt themselves because they feel they are good. Such persons have either forgotten or never truly understood the pit of sin from which they have been rescued (Isaiah 51:1; Psalm 40:2; Isaiah 38:14-20).

The Corinthians felt themselves superior to others because of their wealth and knowledge. Paul the Apostle argued against this attitude in a believer by asking them in 1 Corinthians 4:7: *"For who maketh thee to differ [from another]? and what hast thou that thou didst not receive? now if thou didst receive it, why dost thou glory, as if thou hadst not received it?"* Paul realized that his whole life and salvation had proceeded from the mercy of God. He had no sense of superiority because he knew what a sinner he was. His testimony was, *"This [is] a faithful saying, and worthy of all acceptation, that Christ Jesus came into the world to save sinners; of whom I am chief"* (1 Tim. 1:15). He thus reasoned that since everything was given by God's mercy and initiative that if a person boasted or was proud of anything it would have to be in the Lord and what He had done: *"He that glorieth, let him glory in the Lord"* (1 Cor. 1:27-31; 2 Cor. 10:16-18).

Thus, true repentance is characterized by an appropriate assessment of the crimes committed. It is common today for us to look at how sin affects the people who are sinned against. King David said something quite amazing about this subject. He had seduced Bathsheba and murdered her husband Uriah. Yet, during his confession to God David stated, *"against thee, thee only have I sinned"* (Psalm 51:4). Uriah and Bathsheba might have had something to say about that. They both had definitely been sinned against. Nevertheless, the record is clear that all sin is first and foremost an offense against God and must be dealt with as such.

In our society, a wise man, who doesn't have a leg to stand on in his civil suit, will settle out of court. It is clear that no person on earth will stand a chance of clearing themselves in the court of the LORD. If we are honest, we are undone by his righteousness. We can never measure up to His holy standard. Instead of doing our best, we must admit our personal spiritual bankruptcy and follow the advice of Jesus to settle out of court. When we do, we will find all the mercy and pleasure of heaven will be poured out in our souls and we will have the answer of a clear conscience before God and an assurance of our eternal salvation.

Chapter 5
Avoiding Overestimation

Apparently, people were newshounds in Jesus' day too. They had heard the news about some people from Galilee who had been murdered by Pilate (Luke 13:1-5):

> *There were present at that season some that told him of the Galilaeans, whose blood Pilate had mingled with their sacrifices. And Jesus answering said unto them, Suppose ye that these Galilaeans were sinners above all the Galilaeans, because they suffered such things? I tell you, Nay: but, except ye repent, ye shall all likewise perish. Or those eighteen, upon whom the tower in Siloam fell, and slew them, think ye that they were sinners above all men that dwelt in Jerusalem? I tell you, Nay: but, except ye repent, ye shall all likewise perish.*

These murders by Pilate were a very provocative move. It was an abomination to the devout Jew. Not only were the people killed while worshipping but their worship was then defiled by their own blood being mixed with their sacrifices. It was an act of perverse oppression by a powerful and distinctly unpopular Roman governor.

What was the motive behind someone telling Jesus this news? It seems likely that there was some hope of **provoking** Jesus to act as people thought the expected Messiah should. It could be reasoned that such an outrage should bring about the retribution of an angry God and the expected coming of His Kingdom. That was the expectation of the Jewish people at that time; that Messiah would come to earth, defeat the enemies of Israel and set up his righteous kingdom on earth. Jesus was from Galilee. Certainly this news might somehow motivate Him to seek revenge. This news doesn't seem to be something just spoken of casually but rather, news torn out of the headlines with a purpose to incite rebellion.

This makes Jesus' response even more amazing as we see it in the Gospel account. Rather than take up with popular political discussion, Jesus used this instance to attack an ingrained attitude held amongst the Jewish people and perpetuated by their leaders at that time. The popular teaching about events of such catastrophic proportions, such as the individuals who were murdered, was that they must have been exceptionally evil people. In other words, notwithstanding Pilate's evil deeds, it would be commonly held that the people who died somehow deserved to die as a consequence of some evil they had done at some earlier time in their lives.

This view was reflected both obviously and subtly during the days of Jesus' ministry. The case of the man born blind is one of the most obvious. The disciples sincerely inquired whether it was the man or his parent's fault that he had been born blind. Again, Jesus debunked that kind of thinking and actually stated that the man's blindness was part of God's plan to show His glory the day Jesus healed him: ***"Neither has this man sinned, nor his parent: but that the works of God should be made manifest in him"*** (John 9:3).

In another instance the disciple's tried to incite Jesus to act like Elijah and allow them to call down fire upon those who had rejected His ministry (Luke 9:52-56). The disciples probably held a common Jewish racial bias against Samaritans because they were viewed as racially impure and evil. This was because of the children of Israel's intermarriage in the Northern Kingdom until they became regarded as racially non-Jewish. The disciple's response to the Samaritan rejection seems to reflect the idea that evil people should expect destruction as a consequence of their actions. Jesus stated: *"Ye know not what manner of spirit ye are of. For the son of man is not come to destroy men's lives, but to save them"* (Luke 9:55-56). The desire to see their enemies destroyed reflected an evil attitude.

When people believe that some individuals are worthy of wrath while others are not, there is a sense of moral superiority going on. They are thinking, "Some people are bad but we are good. They got what they deserved and we will get the blessings we deserve." Such moral superiority creates classes of those who deserve judgment and those who do not. The person who believes they are not deserving of God's wrath has woefully overestimated their own goodness. When one feels they are morally superior they will see little need for reflection and repentance. This kind of self-righteousness will then become a profound barrier to finding true repentance or entering God's Kingdom.

That is why Jesus launched into this error of the people with such fervor. Jesus was asking, "Do you really think they deserved it? No way! (Luke 13:2-3)! They didn't deserve to die any more than you do. If they were not right with God when they died they will perish eternally! If you die without repentance you will perish eternally!" Jesus then tore another tragedy from the local headlines: "Those people who were killed when a building fell on them over there in Siloam... were they any different than you? No way! They were just like you! You could be next! You need to repent; now, today!" In the light of eternity and the brevity of life we need to repent when we hear His voice.

Jesus then illustrated this picture of repentance with a parable about what God was doing in Israel then and what He continues to do in our lives now (Luke 13:6-9):

A certain [man] had a fig tree planted in his vineyard; and he came and sought fruit theron, and found none. Then said he unto the dresser of his vineyard, Behold, these three years I come seeking fruit on this fig tree, and find none: cut it down; why cumbereth it the ground? And he answering said unto him, Lord, let it alone this year also, till I shall dig about it, and dung it: And if it bear fruit, well: and if not, then after that thou shalt cut it down.

Notwithstanding the King James language here, the story is pretty simple. The context is the need to repent—Israel's need then and our need now. In this story the point is clear. God may give us more time (digging and fertilizing) or less time to come to repentance but we all have a certain amount of time to become fruitful; then we die… and that's it. If we hear his voice we had better repent immediately.

As we mentioned in an earlier chapter, the Pharisees had an outstanding standard of outward behavior. This caused them to have an attitude of religious superiority—they thought that they were very good. We see this attitude of religious superiority reflected over and over again in the way that they responded to Jesus, His miracles, and His teaching. Their own sense of superiority prevented them from receiving Jesus and His forgiveness because He broke their religious rules. Jesus hung around with 'sinners' of every kind, attended their parties, and even allowed them to touch Him and be in His inner circle.

Today we see all types of denominations and church groups which draw their identities from an externalized effort at holiness. They lay down a 'standard' from the Scripture and demand their adherents 'strive' to attain theses 'standards'. In the best case, such efforts may seem commendable but more often they build that same Pharisaic attitude which looks down upon other people who do not conform to their standards as 'sinners'. They have the same attitude reproved in Scripture: *"Which say, stand by thyself, come not near to me; <u>for I am holier than thou</u> <u>art</u>"* (Isaiah 65:5).

Jesus was very clear about the uselessness of religious efforts and self-recommendation. In Luke 18:9-14, Jesus gave another parable that contrasted those who *"trusted in themselves that they were righteous and despised others"* (v. 9) with those who were able to obtain God's forgiveness and justification. First and foremost, Jesus made a point of telling his audience that the Pharisee was *"praying thus with himself"* (v. 11). What a pathetic picture we are given of a man having a prayer meeting that does not include God. The very point of prayer is to have God hear and answer. Yet, when we fail to properly estimate ourselves, we place ourselves in the same position as this Pharisee— we're just praying with ourselves.

The Pharisee was so involved with himself that he expressed to God his contempt for those who were committing sins that he didn't commit. He expressed his contempt for the publican. He listed for God some of his own activities that he felt made him more righteous than other people. The fact is that this individual didn't see any need to repent of his pride and prejudice. He was so full of himself that he could not see the wickedness of his comparisons and assertions. His overestimation of himself meant that he would have these conversations with himself over and over again and never be right with God.

In contrast, the publican was weighted down with his sin. He couldn't even bring himself to look up toward heaven (v. 13) but kept hitting himself on the chest because of his internal conviction. He cried out to God for forgiveness from his sins. HE FELT THE WEIGHT OF HIS SIN. He was sorrowful with a godly sorrow. He confessed his sins to God. He really had changed his mind about his life of sin. He went away from the Temple justified!

This can be a very slippery slope for the churchgoer. Many start out grieving over some of the things that they have done. They may be sick and tired of certain particular sins that have ruined their lives and dragged them down. There is a tendency in all of us to forget the pit of sin that we have come from. Once God takes away our sin, we tend to start to feel pretty good about ourselves. We can then be fooled into thinking that **we** had something to do with the transformation that has begun in our lives. Many people end up acting very religious and they start to look down upon other people who seem to struggle or fall into public disgrace. I heard of a Bible College professor who always told his students that, "Each of us have a little Pharisee inside of us just waiting to get out!" He was absolutely right.

Pride is the shining star that blinds so many who have gone some distance along the Way. The original sin of Lucifer was that he exalted himself toward being equal with God: *"I will"* (Isaiah 14:12-14; Eze. 28:2-6). He later tempted Eve with the same thing: *"ye shall be as gods"* (Gen. 3:5). This is the direction that the devil wants to go with us, too. He wants our 'I' to be exalted in the place of God. If the devil can get us to kick God off the throne of our heart we are already aligned with his kingdom. Exalting our 'self' is the root of what we call original sin. When we finally see this truth applies to us, we will want to repent, *"in ashes"* (Jer. 6:26; Jonah 3:6-10).

In 2 Cor. 10:12 The Apostle Paul said:

For we dare not make ourselves of the number, or compare ourselves with some that commend themselves: but they measuring themselves by themselves, and comparing themselves among themselves, are not wise.

This Scripture has saved my life so many times. You cannot read this Scripture without seeing that comparison with others is futile. Paul was talking about some people who were his opponents when he wasn't in Corinth. They compared their ministry to his to puff themselves up. This is the essence of self-righteousness and deceit. When I look on another with the mind to feel better about myself, I put myself in a very dangerous place. If I assess myself in any other way than in relation to God's Word, I will fall into error.

God's Word declares us all sinners. *"All have sinned and come short of the glory of God"* (Romans 3:23). Every one of us is a part of all. I am saved by His grace. I have no work to recommend me to the most High. We never move out of that position because anything that we 'do' in the Kingdom of God comes by the power of God's Holy Spirit and His Word working in us. Concerning the fact that we are new creatures in God, Paul the Apostle tells us in 2 Cor. 5:18: *"all things are of God, who hath reconciled us to himself by Jesus Christ, and hath given to us the ministry of reconciliation"*! The bragging Christian or the self-righteous Christian is an oxy-moron. Everything we will ever be or do proceeds from God.

Jesus gives us the appropriate response to the times when we are having a 'heyday' and we have successful days. Jesus said, *"So likewise ye, when ye shall have done*

***all those things which are commanded you, say, we are
unprofitable servants: We have done that which was our
duty to do.*** *"* (Luke 17:10). What an amazing mindset, yet it
is a key to success in God's Kingdom. It is appropriate
self-assessment. The context of this comment was Jesus'
reminder that servants don't get standing ovations for being
servants. That is their job. If we would only understand
our weakness, our need to grow, and how proud we have
been, there would be more room for God's government in
our lives.

We really can't apply this lesson to others but each of
us may apply it to ourselves. Ultimately, I am the only one
that I can do anything about. Too many people look around
at others like the Pharisee who prayed with himself. Their
assessment of others warps their assessment of themselves.
If the truth is to be told, I need to repent! I need miracles of
forgiveness and deliverance. I need to feel angst, to smite
my breast, to cry out—because I am bankrupt. Each of us
is. We are lower than beggars; we are bankrupts who have
nothing to bring to God, except ourselves. Jesus was very
clear that without Him we could do nothing (John 15:5).
Anything else is a gross over-estimation.

Chapter 6
Coming In On Budget

Many years ago I decided to be the general contractor for the construction of my own house. A few of the fellows that I worked with had built there own homes and had all kinds of tales about cost over-runs and do-it-yourself jobs that were never really completed. I obtained a self-help book and meticulously priced out ever aspect of the job. It was clear that my co-workers were very bright guys but had not really sat down and anticipated all of the expenses and potential changes that might come up. Some of them came in twenty, thirty or even fifty percent over budget when their homes were completed. I really learned from their mistakes and came in less than seven percent over budget with the house being completed in just eleven weeks. My success had come from appropriately anticipating and counting the cost of the entire project.

Jesus was a contractor who never sinned! In Luke 14:28-30, Jesus asked a question that He, as a professional builder, could draw upon from personal experience:

> *For which of you, intending to build a tower, sitteth not down first, and counteth the cost, whether he have sufficient to finish it? Lest haply, after he hath laid the foundation, and is not able to finish it, all that behold it begin to mock him, Saying, This man began to build, and was not able to finish.*

Jesus acknowledged that there is a measure of humiliation involved with not completing a public work. In this present world it just makes sense to sit down and efficiently figure out what a large project will cost because we have many examples of the humiliation incurred when a project is way over budget or just cannot be completed.

Jesus gave this illustration to His followers immediately after calling upon them to hate even the closest family tie that would hinder them from appropriately serving in the Kingdom of God (Luke 14:26-27). He further stated that the very expenditure of the time of our lives must be subjugated to the rule of His Kingdom. He then added to this self-denial the new activity of the Kingdom: cross-bearing. There is no doubt that such claims brought all manner of wonder and consternation to His followers. Jesus had no desire to mitigate His claims. Rather, He gave us another picture of repentance; that of ruthless self-examination. Our goal is to determine whether we really fully desire to enter His Kingdom or whether we are not willing to pay what is required to enter in.

In our day, many people are invited to receive Christ without being given any fair kind of presentation of the claims He makes on the human soul. This gives us a particular problem at this present time. Many people in the institutional church have never sat down to count the cost of entering into God's Kingdom. They were told that salvation was absolutely free and that they need 'do' nothing to be saved. In stark contrast, Jesus taught that, far beyond quitting the sin business, an individual must even happily yield up to God that which this present world regards as sacred: family ties and friends. It appears that ignoring Jesus' claims disqualifies one from entering the Kingdom of God. Repentance must be accompanied by a great over-riding conviction and determination that nothing will be held back from the rule of the King. Jesus counsels all seekers to stop and think about what they are doing.

I want to be clear that I am not talking about the practice of many who use these verses to encourage human effort to achieve godliness. We are to strive to enter the straight gate (Matt. 7:13-14). That gate is the gate of Jesus Christ. Only He can allow us entry into the fellowship of His rule and reign in our lives. The only hope for our subsequent obedience to our heavenly Father is the empowering grace that His rule in a human heart can give. All of the ability comes from God's rule in an individual's heart. Therefore, one is not working to gain Father's approval but rather they are laboring to yield to His indwelling Kingdom, to enter His rest (Heb. 4:10-11). All that we will ever be—*"every good and perfect gift"*— comes out of the heavens *"from the Father of Lights, with whom is no variableness, neither shadow of turning"* (James 1:17).

Jesus' building illustration clearly shows that the builder started construction. He **wanted** to complete the building but did not have the materials to finish. There was an initial enthusiasm, a flurry of action. This poor fellow ran out of money before he could even start the framing process and what was left was wasted and mocked. I remember such a project in one subdivision that I lived in that looked exactly like this picture. A contractor had started the project but got only as far as the foundation before he ran out of money. Over a period of years the lot became overgrown to the point that one could just barely make out the abandoned foundation. Unless the new owner intended to build the identical house they would have to break up the foundation and start over again.

Today, we wonder why so many people will show an interest in Jesus but soon fade away into their former state or just go to church and endeavor to be 'religious". Jesus' clear explanation is that they never counted the cost of following Him. When they were called upon to pay some price for His Kingdom they were unwilling or unable to do so. It seems likely that many who profess to know Christ never truly counted the cost and were never able to truly repent. Since they had never really been regenerated, they 'tried' to be religious, building their spiritual house in their own way.

Next, Jesus used a more serious illustration: War! War costs men their lives and kings their kingdoms. There are winners and losers. The results are final. Jesus speaks of a king who is hopelessly outmatched by an opposing king. He only has half of the standing army of the king that is coming to do battle with him. The Jewish people could readily relate to this scenario. They had been outmatched and dominated for some time by the occupying Romans. The Roman occupiers worked consistently to crush all rebellion and insurgency with their superior manpower and armaments.

Jesus took it as an obvious fact that any sensible king who has half the army of one that is coming up against him will appropriately measure the consequences of going to war with a superior foe and act accordingly. Notice that the king sends out his ambassadors while his enemy is still *"yet a great way off"* (Luke 14:32). The point is clear: the person who would decide for Jesus must seek out the facts concerning Christ's claims upon their life, reflect carefully upon Christ's claims, and make a decision based on serious reflection and conviction. I have repeatedly seen the success of those who come to Christ under great conviction of sin. They have come under a great conviction of a need to 'sell out' to God.

Perhaps people who have not counted the cost are the people Jesus is talking about as the *"stony ground"* people in the parable of the soils (Mark 4:1-20). *"Stony ground"* people are happy to hear about Jesus and His Kingdom. Unfortunately, they have not realized or counted the cost of receiving the Word of the Kingdom. Sunshine is absolutely essential in agriculture. It is what makes seeds germinate and sprout. Jesus tells us that troubles of all kinds and persecutions are His sunshine. These are the very things that will make His Word sprout in a believer's life. Conversely, these are the very things that will shrivel a stony (shallow) ground person. It is clear that they had never really counted on all kinds of trouble, so when it arrives (as it most assuredly will), they quit and fade into churchy religion or return to their former state.

Preceding Jesus' command to count the cost in Luke 14:25-27, Jesus told a story about a man who made a feast (Luke 14:16-24). Ed Corley's exposition of this passage includes the fact that this is the last meal of the day. The story in Matthew 22:1-14 is different. It refers to a king whose feast is earlier in the day. Rev. Corley thinks that the Matthew account refers to the Jewish people and Jesus' attempt to bring His Kingdom to them. He believes that the later account in Luke refers to those in the professing church in the very last days that are bidden to participate in Christ's Kingdom and reach the lost. The professing church people were too busy (vv. 18-20). The Lord then sends His servants out into the *"highways and the hedges"* (v. 23). The servants who were unavailable were rejected. They were replaced by the willing beggars in the streets.

In the Luke account the response is the same as Matthew. The telling comment is made in Luke 14:18: *"and they all began with one consent to make excuse"*. One gentleman had bought land that he hadn't seen, so he had to go and look at it. Another had bought oxen he hadn't seen and was going to make sure they were good. Another was married and 'honey' wanted him home. That makes two fools and a wimp. Only a fool buys something 'sight-unseen' and only a wimp will hide behind their marital relationship to excuse themselves from an obligation. They didn't have reasons, only excuses.

From what circumstance did these excuses arise? These people had undervalued their friendship with the powerful man (God) who invited them (v. 16). They had other things to do that they valued over and above this man's friendship. The cost was too great and when they were called upon by their friend, they had something else to do. They had not sat down and calculated the cost of their relationship with their friend or the cost of missing that special meal. There is no doubt that it cost them to lose their friendship with this man, along with its benefits. Today, in exactly the same way, many in the professing church have undervalued the King and His Kingdom. They are too busy when He calls and must begin, one by one, to make excuse. They never sat down and counted the cost of having a relationship with the King.

As we mentioned earlier, Jesus presented a cross to His followers. Although nobody had conceived that Jesus was to become the atoning sacrifice for sin upon a cross, nobody could miss the symbolism. There were all manner of executions outside of Jerusalem. Crucifixion was the preferred method. Instead of making it easy for people to come to Him, Jesus set up seemingly impossible barriers to following Him. He demanded our all, our complete devotion, as a condition of entering into the Kingdom of God.

Unless one pressed into the Kingdom with single-minded devotion and vigor they would not succeed in entering it because: ***"from the days of John the Baptist until now the kingdom of heaven suffereth violence, and the violent take it by force*** (Matt. 11:12). Jesus made it clear that we must not enter into this life-consuming endeavor without sitting down and carefully counting the cost of our decision. Jesus wanted no religious dilettantes.

If you are reading this, you may be offended. Your mind may cry out, "Too much!" You may have been in church for many years and be a very nice religious person but now realize that you have never really sat down and examined the claims of the King or this Kingdom. It would be wise to study carefully all that Jesus said about following Him and carefully weigh the cost of serving Him against the cost of His eternal wrath and judgment. Although such reflection is sobering, it is also useful for restoring perspective and preparing us to truly 'sell out' to God.

There is a word of hope to the religious churchgoer who needs a revolution in their heart and life. Both Isaiah and Hosea use an agricultural picture to help us understand what is needed: breaking up the *"fallow ground"* of our heart (Jer. 4:1-5; Hos. 10:12). Fallow refers to ground that has been left alone from agriculture. The natural vegetation takes over and the ground becomes very hard. The only solution to make it useful is to break it open. This is much harder than regular plowing because there will be places in a fallow field that one must stop and break up by hand. If the ground is not properly broken up, it will never plough properly and will never bring forth an appropriate harvest.

There is hope for the backslider then, and so many are backsliders because the Scripture states: *"The backslider in heart shall be filled with his own ways"* (Prov. 14:14). The backslider is just doing what they want rather than what Jesus wants. The exhortation to break up the fallow ground tells me that I can become involved with changing the state of the ground of my heart. If I have become hard and settled in my ways, I can allow God to tenderize and soften me so that I might truly appreciate His claims upon me and His commandments to me. This will break up all of my excuses for not doing what He has told me. Instead I will be able to say, ***"Speak Lord, for thy servant heareth"*** (1 Sam. 3:9-10).

We can count the cost now or pay the price later. As the songwriter A. J. Hodge wrote many years ago:

> Have you counted the cost?
> If your soul should be lost?
> Though you gain
> The whole world for your own.
> Even now it may be,
> That line you have crossed.
> Have you counted?
> Have you counted the cost?

Friend, count the cost and pay the price. Eternity is a very long time.

Chapter 7

Pay Up!

We all know people who have incurred debts, made commitments to pay for something, or have promised to give something, only to later renege on their obligation. It is one thing to say that we are willing to do something but it is quite another to follow through and do it. Not only does Jesus demand of His followers that they count the cost of following Him but once the cost is calculated they are commanded to pay the full price. Jesus gives a number of pictures of what it takes to follow through on our commitment to His Kingdom with singleness of mind and purpose. It is clear that nothing short of single-minded devotion will enter the Kingdom of God.

In Matt. 13:44-46, Jesus gives two little parables that illustrate how we may enter God's Kingdom:

> *Again, the kingdom of heaven is like unto treasure hid in a field; the which when a man hath found, he hideth, and for joy thereof goeth and selleth all that he hath, and buyeth that field. Again, the kingdom of heaven is like unto a merchant man, seeking goodly pearls: Who, when he had found one pearl of great price, went and sold all that he had, and bought it.*

You do not need to be a clever theologian to understand the thrust of both parables. They are both about 'selling out'.

Just before these two parables, Jesus had told his audience the Parable of the Wheat and the Weeds (Matt. 13:24-30). Afterwards, when Jesus was alone with the disciples He told them that the weeds and the wheat grew up together so that the wheat wouldn't be destroyed (Matt. 13:36-43). Those who are justified by faith in Jesus are being saved and becoming fruitful, generation after generation. Jesus promises that at the end of the age there will be a judgment. There will be an abject difference between the fate of the children of the Kingdom and the children of the evil one.

Right after the two little parables, Jesus gave another parable to reinforce the Parable of the Wheat and the Weeds. This is the Parable of the Fishing Net (Matt. 13:47-50). While there are many more helpful details in the Parable of the Wheat and the Weeds, the Parable of the Fishing Net reinforces only one point—judgment. Jesus speaks about the gathering and separation of the useful and useless fish as well as the useful wheat and the useless weeds. Their fate is profoundly different. In the first parable Jesus contrasts the state of the just who *"shine forth as the sun"* with the pitiful state of those who continue in iniquity who are *"wailing and gnashing"* their teeth (v. 42). In the second parable of the fishes, Jesus only reiterates the state of those who are outside the Kingdom: *"wailing and gnashing"* (v. 50).

Jesus clearly wanted to impress upon the disciples the teaching of eternal judgment. In the midst of this teaching, Jesus gave the two parallel illustrations of how one may **avoid** this judgment. Both the parable of the Treasure in the Field and of the Pearl of Great Price, drive home the same point. Both individuals calculated that they had only enough to purchase the object of their desire. Most importantly, both individuals did what was necessary to liquidate their assets and then followed through with the deal. There is a profound determination lurking beneath the surface of both stories. Both men displayed a single-minded fanaticism to get what they wanted. They were obsessed and had to possess their treasures. They somehow got the money for their prizes and 'paid up'.

In the light and context of eternal judgment anyone who regards the Kingdom of God as the treasure or the pearl to be possessed, is displaying twenty-twenty vision into eternal things. Jesus is driving home a central point—there must be a **singleness of purpose** in entering into the Kingdom of Heaven. No obstacle may be tolerated in our pursuit of God. We must have Him, to the exclusion of everything. There is no doubt that this is what Jesus means. In the light of what is attained—entrance into the Kingdom—it is a value-added investment indeed. Such investment is another picture of repentance.

But what does this have to do with repentance? It is simple: instruction. One who has truly repented will have, as their single focus, the Kingdom and glory of God. This singleness of mind might be called a 'symptom' of having repented in the first place. It is clear that we cannot enter the Kingdom by our own effort, righteousness or initiative. Jesus clearly taught: *"No man can come to me, except the Father which hath sent me draw him: and I will raise him up at the last day."* (John 6:44).

Yet, paradoxically, each man who is drawn to Jesus must respond **when they hear His voice** (Psalm 95:7, 8; Heb. 3:7-8, 15; 4:7). This fact is an absolute key to finding repentance. In a very real way, salvation is a 'right now' kind of thing because: *"behold, now is the accepted time; behold, now is the day of salvation."* (2 Cor. 6:2; see also Isaiah 49:8). The salvation of God is pressed upon men by the Holy Spirit: *"And when he is come, he will reprove the world of sin, and of righteousness, and of judgment:"* (John 16:8). When we hear His voice we need to respond in season. The idea of doing it later leaves all of the power of salvation at the beck and call of men. This concept is not in concert with the Scriptures. When God's message is given to a person it is given with an urgency that demands a response.

Whether our answer to God is 'yes' or 'no', our heart does not remain static—it either becomes harder or softer towards God. The Writer of Hebrews exhorts his audience: *"Wherefore, (As the Holy Ghost saith, To day if ye will hear his voice, Harden not your hearts, as in the provocation, in the day of temptation in the wilderness..."* (Heb. 3:7-8). He repeats this theme two more times. There are times when God calls. The Bible teaches that there is a time when God stops calling. His Word says: *"My spirit shall not always strive with man."* (Gen. 6:3). No man can know when the Lord will cease calling. That is why God has warned us to respond when we hear Him.

One of the measures or plumb-lines of repentance is the conviction with which an individual enters into it and continues in it. The repentant person may sin. They may struggle with certain sins, even for years. They may despair of themselves. Nevertheless, they are marked with a permanently changed attitude towards sin. They will acknowledge it as sin and seek to be conformed to the expressed image of God's will.

There are a vast number of Scriptures that teach that the truly repentant person will overcome their sin. One of the most clear and compelling is 1 John 5:2-5:

By this we know that we love the children of God, when we love God, and keep his commandments. For this is the love of God, that we keep his commandments: and his commandments are not grievous. For whatsoever is born of God overcometh the world: and this is the victory that overcometh the world, even

68

our faith.   Who is he that <u>overcometh the world</u>, but
he that believeth that Jesus is the Son of God?

In the Apostle John's mind the true mark of the repentant
believer was that they quit persisting in a lifestyle of sin
and allowed the government of God to conform them to His
image.

Do you see that John associated the love of God and
faith in God to obedience to His will? Many will excuse
themselves from repenting from sin because they are
persuaded that God loves them "just as they are". Nothing
could be further from the truth. When we repent, Christ
will receive us just as we are but will then begin His work
of transformation into being **just like He is**. Jesus' work is
all about getting rid of sin in our lives. As well, the essence
of faith is to obey Christ.   It is this obedience to the
commandments of Jesus that prove both our love for God
and our faith in God.

Another picture of this singleness of mind was the
Ancient Farmer (Luke 9:60-62). In response to the excuse
of a would-be follower that they needed to go home and
deal with family matters Jesus said: *"No man, having put
his hand to the plough, and looking back, is fit for the
kingdom of God."* It is likely that this individual was asking more of Jesus than to say a farewell. Perhaps he was
going home to set his affairs in order and give instructions
concerning his business. It may well have been that he was
going home to 'check' with family and friends, providing
for himself an opportunity to be dissuaded.

Whatever the man's motive, Jesus saw a potential
excuse or departure in the request. If we look objectively at
what was requested, Jesus' response is still quite
astonishing. This is especially true when we look at the
man's request in the light of the foreign interests that we

69

allow to be intermingled with our presentation of the claims of Christ. Jesus basically responded, "No! That will simply not do". Even such legitimate preparation with hesitation was enough to miss entering into the Kingdom. We would think someone quite harsh to dismiss a sincere inquirer so quickly today but Jesus' call was for an absolute commitment.

The use of the horse and plough is obsolete nowadays. It is safe to say that very few farmers in modern-day America know how to cut the ground with a hand-plough pulled by an ox. It is hard to convey to our mind the concentration that is necessary to cut a straight furrow for planting. One must aim the plough at a point in the distance and direct it very skillfully in a straight line. It is impossible to do this effectively while your attention is directed elsewhere. The full focus of the farmer must be on ploughing and the full focus of the son of the Kingdom must be on allowing the King to rule in their entire life. Repentance brings God's government as the sole focus in a person's life.

An appropriate way to understand this is by thinking about intention. I am not talking about the passing fancies and surface feelings that form so many people's decisions and govern their lifestyles. A good ploughman has a single intention. His desire is to cut each furrow as straight as possible. When he starts ploughing, he may have mistakes, halts, turns, and the like. Nevertheless, as the years go by, his skill is honed by repetition and concentration. Focus is the key. He has a strong and fixed intention that he brings to a reality. The result is straight furrows.

Similarly, another very small and ominous statement by Jesus belies a very enlightening story from the Biblical record. In the midst of a discourse about the coming trouble to the Jewish people after his ascension and the difficulties His followers would endure, Jesus commented cryptically, *"Remember Lot's wife"* (Luke 7:32). This is a reference to the tragic story of Lot's emergency departure from Sodom with only his wife and unmarried daughters (Gen. 19). Lot's wife lingered while she longed for Sodom and looked back, against the direct instructions of the angels (v. 16). She was destroyed by the outpouring of sulfurous fire from heaven and became encrusted in salt.

It is very interesting that Peter refers to Lot as *"just Lot, vexed with the filthy conversation of the wicked"* (2 Peter 2:7). The record of his behavior does not seem very just as it is recorded in Genesis 19. He offered the angry homosexual mob that came to rape his angelic guests his two virgin daughters (v. 8). He had been warned of the imminent judgment from God and yet lingered with grief over Sodom for so long that the angels had to drag him, his wife, and two daughters to the outskirts of town (v. 16). Later, no doubt grief-stricken over the loss of his married daughters and his wife, he allowed himself to become so drunk that he submitted to sexual relations with his two unmarried daughters (vv. 31-38).

Lot's decision to take his family and pitch his tent near Sodom was a grave error (Gen. 13:12). He eventually moved into the city and was overcome, to a large extent, by their lifestyle. Although it is clear that he did not partici-pate in the debauchery that was going on in Sodom, he loved the place. So did Mrs. Lot. Her affection for her associations, family, and possessions in Sodom was fatal. Jesus uses this cryptic word to warn us not to be so affected. Our focus must be singly toward God's King-dom. We must repent of our own particular love for this present world system because the whole realm is opposed to God: *"Love not the world, neither the things that are in* *the world. If <u>any man</u> love the world, the love of the Father is not in him."* (1 John 2:15).

This is what the old-timers used to mean by being sold out. My friend Ed Corley says that nobody can tell you, "the price of buying the field" (Matt.13:44). Only God can tell each person what the price is between them and Him. It is certain that placing an appropriately high value on God's Kingdom over and above anything in this world or life is a central part of Biblical repentance. Jesus repeatedly stressed the need to be single-minded in our quest to enter into His Kingdom. No price is too great because: *"we brought nothing into this world, and it is certain that we can carry nothing out"* (1 Tim. 6:7). In response to the multiple exhortations of the Bible to be sold out to God it would be wise for us to take Mary's advice: *"Whatsoever he saith unto you, do it"* (John 2:5). You will be glad you did.

Chapter 8
The Greatest In The Kingdom

In a previous chapter we saw the great danger of overestimating ourselves. Jesus has given us another way that will lead to greatness and increase in His Kingdom. This is the way of humility. Although I may humble myself, it is humility that is built into me by the indwelling Kingdom of God that qualifies me to do great things in Christ's Kingdom.

The Scripture speaks of *"voluntary humility"* (Col. 2:18). This may be better translated "taking delight in their humility". The idea is that we pretend to be humble; that a man produces humility in an attempt to please and be like God. In contrast, true godly humility is worked through a man who has seen himself for what he is and who has seen Christ for who He is.

There is a very interesting flow to the events that are recorded in Chapters Sixteen to Eighteen of the Book of Matthew. This is the place we see the type of person qualified to lead in the Kingdom of God. The main characteristic of someone who aspires to lead is very simple—godly humility. Here Jesus gives us a profound picture of repentance.

In the Sixteenth Chapter of Matthew we see Jesus shift gears in His ministry. Jesus asked the disciples who men were saying He was. Then Jesus asked the disciples who they said He was (vv. 13-17). Peter answered that Jesus was the Messiah, the son of God. Jesus acknowledged that this was a divine revelation. Jesus used a play on words between Peter, whose name meant pebble, and Himself as the Foundation Rock. Jesus was revealing that He would build the 'called out ones' (Church) upon Himself (v. 18).

Jesus then mentioned the authority of the future Body of Christ (v. 19) which he later expanded upon in Matthew 18:18-20. Jesus told them to tell no one that He was the Christ and revealed the means of bringing in His Kingdom—His death on the Cross (vv. 20-23). Peter could not receive that new truth. Even though he was the person who had the revelation of Jesus as Messiah, Jesus had to rebuke Peter for being aligned with Satan. Jesus then told them that all of His followers would take up their own crosses, not loving their own lives and would follow Him (vv.24-27). Finally, He alluded to His coming Transfiguration (v. 28).

Matthew Seventeen starts out with Matthew's account of the Transfiguration (vv. 1-13). Peter, James, and John actually saw Jesus in His glory. Upon coming down from the mountain Jesus is greeted with the disciple's first recorded failure to deliver someone in Jesus' name (vv. 14-21). Jesus gave the disciples some insight into what I call the 'fasted' lifestyle—spiritual preparation for spiritual warfare. The disciples had obviously not been participating in a lifestyle of self-denial (vv. 19-21). Thus, when push came to shove, they had no faith for the task at hand—delivering the demonized child. Jesus then reiterated the necessity of His future sacrifice on the Cross (vv. 22-23).

We see all of these events culminate in Matthew Eighteen. The disciples had heard and seen enough to realize that things were coming to a head. In spite of all of Jesus' allusions to denial of self and the death of the Cross, it seems that the disciples were convinced that Jesus was about to bring the Kingdom of Heaven down to earth so they asked, ***"Who is greatest in the kingdom of heaven?"*** (v. 1). This is really a 'brass tacks' kind of question: "Alright Jesus, who is going to be in charge around here?" We know their motive was to be leaders because later

James and John (with the help of their mommy) would ask for the preeminent positions at the left and right hand of Jesus when He came to rule in His Kingdom (Matt. 20:20). They were not being vague in their question but clearly were wondering who among them would be in charge.

At this point, much closer to the end of His ministry on earth and headed to the Cross, Jesus again referred to another essential aspect of repentance—humility (vv. 1-5). Jesus placed a very small child in the middle of the group and basically said, "This is what a leader in My Kingdom will look like." Standing in opposition to the person who over-assesses their spiritual state, Jesus recommended properly assessing our spiritual state. Jesus told them they must be converted (literally: 'turned around') to even enter God's Kingdom. This turning can only be accomplished by a complete turn of mind toward God—repentance. Although Jesus had started His ministry preaching repentance (Matt. 4:17) it is clear that, with all of their faithfulness and sacrifice, the disciple's hearts had not been really 'turned' to God.

What an abject and shocking illustration a little child was for those big men who were ready to lead. What is it about an infant that Jesus was referring to? Jesus is clear that His main thrust was humility. A little child has no power, place, or status. They have not learned the clever presentation of a false persona. Their world is simple, not complex. They are not sophisticated (it is interesting that the archaic use of the word sophistication used to refer to corruption). Children have not learned to love vain things. Infants love, trust, and depend on their parents. Ultimately, little children are content with their lot. As long as they have their basic needs, and love, they are content to have fun and play. Infants trust their parents implicitly.

Jesus was telling us that we must humble ourselves **as** a child. He is referring to what His Kingdom will do as it advances in a person's life. Having repented or turned means a person will have admitted their bankruptcy with regards to producing a godly life. As they submit themselves to sanctification, they will be stripped of more and more of the 'grown up' baloney that passes for the adult life. Their humble dependence on Jesus, day by day, will cause them to draw their security and their identity from Him. Such humble lives will become so simple that they will seem extreme to those around them. As they grow in grace they will be able to, *"Be... followers of God, as dear children;"* (Eph. 5:1). It is only the great process of change that God brings that can make a person so humble.

Today, most of the professing church has the same problem as the disciples did. While we may give mental assent to the idea of being a 'servant' we only go a little way with it. I have heard many who come under life's pressures say: "I have my limits! After all I'm a King's kid and He hasn't called me to be anybody's doormat!" Who wants to be a doormat slave? In this present day we see all kinds of people in the church who would have us submit to them but show little of this kind of self-denying humility. According to this standard, the greatest people in the Kingdom of God may well be hidden away and little known. In our fame-crazed time it just doesn't seem to make sense to, *"humble yourselves therefore under the mighty hand of God that he may exalt you in due time"* (1 Peter 5:6). Nevertheless, godly humility and repentance go hand in hand.

The humble infant as a type of those who are great is carried forward into a continued exposition by Jesus. Jesus speaks of the danger of offending the *"little ones"* (Matt.

18:6-10). Is it children that Jesus is talking about? It obviously is not just children, judging by the teaching that follows. Jesus warns those who believe not to offend child-like Christians from their faith in God. The word offend comes from the Greek *skandalizo* which is the root of our English word scandal. Jesus is not speaking of upsetting or bothering fussy people. Neither is Jesus trying to get us to mitigate the offensive aspects of His message or call.

Jesus is speaking of casting stumbling-blocks in other believer's paths that cause them to veer from the path of God. Jesus' teaching becomes an exposition about the lengths a humble follower of Jesus will need to go in order not to stumble others. Jesus recommends suicide over causing the humble believer to stumble and fall (v. 6). That is troublingly extreme! What motivated Jesus' comments? He wanted those who would follow Him to wake up to the eternal consequences of their life in the world.

Jesus went on to reiterate what he taught earlier in His ministry during the Sermon on the Mount—to tear out the eye or limb that drags us away into sin (Matt. 5:29-30; 18:8-9). Again, this is another extreme illustration that His people must live carefully. Obviously, self-mutilation will not deal with the inner lusts that cause a man to sin and become a stumbling-block. Christ's Kingdom will deal ruthlessly with evil in any disciple's personal life. The violence of the conviction goes so deep that the disciple would pluck an eye or cut off a hand, if such practices could actually deliver a person from doing evil.

Why? The Kingdom of God that comes into a man's heart will bring a far reaching, humble, self-examination and self-denial. These are essential to a successful repentance from sin. It is a Christian principle that: *"... none of us liveth to himself, and no man dieth to himself."* (Romans 14:7). Paul was talking about people's convictions concerning diet. The whole context of Romans Fourteen was looking out for the conscience of others and seeing that we don't cause them to stumble or be scandalized. We are not to judge those who have convictions that we may think go too far. It is part of God's love (*agape*) to live with an eye for the weakness of those around us. The repentant soul is not seeking their 'rights' but the good edification of all those around them.

Looking out for others goes deeper still. Ruthlessness with the roots of our sins and selfishness will save us. The person willing to be so ruthless will be changed by the power of God while those who are not willing to be so ruthless with themselves will taste of eternal hellfire (vv. 8-10). It must be true that we are **able** to deal with the roots of sin in our lives or Jesus would never have told us to do so.

Further, we must deal with any hatred that we might feel towards these "little ones" if the purity of their life reproves us. This is why John deals with this *agape* love that comes from being *"born of God"* so extensively in First John. It is both the diagnostic and the cure for sin. Jesus tells us to watch out for hate as we are being led by the Lord through this sanctifying process (Matt. 18:10). Hate is poison to the deliverance of an individual from evil habits and motives.

Jesus then stated that His Kingdom is motivated by rescue (Matt. 18: 11)! He used the illustration of the shepherd who leaves the sheep to seek high and low for the lost sheep (Matt. 18:12-14). This then becomes an essential mindset for those of us who are little ones. We are His representatives, seeking to publish all of His truth abroad and rescue every fallen brother who fails. Rather than ruling, as the disciples had desired to do, we are to be in alignment with the heart of the King who came to *"seek and save that which was lost"* (Luke 19:10; Matt. 18:11).

This comes first through our sanctification into the will of God and next by our laying hold of this rescuing attitude toward our brethren and the world in general.

Jesus became more specific about the care required in our relationships with other believers. This is the part of Matthew Eighteen that people seem to know but they don't seem to understand the context. We are to follow the guidelines that Jesus laid out for dealing with sin because we are ourselves repentant (Matt. 18: 15-17). We have God's heavenly rescue attitude. We want to successfully participate in the power of the Kingdom. Rather than speak to everyone else when someone hurts us, we speak to the offending party. If we are unsuccessful we bring one or two witnesses. Then we are to bring the matter before the fellowship of believers with which we are associated. Our whole motive is love and rescue because we are concerned when our brethren fall into sin.

We are to deal with people this way because we ourselves have sinned. We desire mercy because we have been shown mercy. We want to protect another person from undue censure, so we keep the matter just between us and the other person. We are also very interested in keeping up the good testimony of our fellowship as it represents Christ in the world. This is the loving way to deal with the situation.

Finally, we have bigger fish to fry! If we are consistently taken up with sin and offense we will never be able to fulfill our mandate to represent God in the world by corporate prayer, spiritual warfare, evangelism, and Christian fellowship. Our business as the Body of Christ in the world is too important to be given up for vindication from offense or indulgence in sin.

In reality, Jesus took the question of 'who's in charge?' to His own logical conclusion. His entire dialogue is illustrating the need for spiritually bankrupt men to allow the government of His Kingdom to rule in their hearts so that His love, concern, holiness, and will, might be expressed in the world. Our bickering about leadership is just as much a problem today as it was amongst the disciples. Jesus has no need for us to lead—He is quite capable of doing it. The indwelling Holy Spirit gave such fine direction to the First Century Church that they were able to say in their letter to the new Gentile believers: *"For it seemed good to the Holy Ghost, and to us,"* (Acts 15:28).

The point, then, is that repentance brings godly humility which brings *agape* (the love that comes from God). No man has *agape* because its only source is the heavenly Father. The Scripture tells us that: *"the love of God is shed abroad in our hearts by the holy ghost which is given unto us"* (Romans 5:5). We don't have this love! We cannot produce it. We must receive it and we may only do so if we repent of our pride and self-will and allow God to rule. When God rules, His love flows. Conversely, there is no *agape* when God doesn't rule.

Matthew 18:18-20 illustrates that the humility which God imparts to us qualifies us to be effectual in His Kingdom:

> *Verily I say unto you, Whatsoever ye shall bind on earth shall be bound in heaven: and whatsoever ye shall loose on earth shall be loosed in heaven. Again I say unto you, That if two of you shall agree on earth as touching any thing that they shall ask, it shall be done for them of my Father which is in heaven. For where two or three are gathered together in my name, there am I in the midst of them.*

As few as two or three who are thus unified in the humility of being a 'little one' may then participate in the government of God.

This is why we must live a life of God-inspired humility, purity, unselfishness, rescue, and restoration. Our business is far too great for a partial repentance. We must go all the way. Then we will **bind and loose** things in the heavens. We will **come into an agreement** that will produce profound answers to prayer. We will experience the **Presence of Jesus** in our midst. Really, we must repent. We do so not only for our own good but for the good of everyone we know and for the advancement of God's Kingdom. Humble repentance is truly an act of love, both to our Father and to everyone we know.

These three promises become a *"threefold cord"* that *"is not quickly broken"* (Eccl. 4:12). The power, unity, and fellowship promised by Jesus can only be given to those who are humble and completely yielded to His purposes. Those who have fully repented will be blessed to *"see God"* (Matt. 5:8); not with human eyes but the eyes of their hearts. They will be able to apprehend the promised heavenly results because God will gift them with a pure assurance that they are the children of God. What a motivation for the saints to seek the place of humility and service. This is the place where Christ's Body will produce 'God results'.

While we do not want to produce phony humility the Bible clearly teaches that we have a part in finding the place of humility. We are told that: *"God resisteth the proud, but giveth grace to the humble"* (James 4:6; 1 Peter 4:5). If we humble ourselves and learn to depend on God's grace, God will draw near to us. Paul the Apostle asks: *"Where is boasting then? It is excluded. By what law? Of works? Nay: but by the law of faith"* (Romans 3:27).

It is faith that is given to us as a gift that saves us. This means that the proud Christian is an oxymoron. The true penitent will always be humble and agree with Paul who concludes: ***"He that glorieth, let him glory in the Lord"*** (1 Cor. 1:31; 2 Cor. 10:17).

Chapter 9
Death Begets Life

One of the great seeming paradoxes of the Christian life is Christ's call to come and die. As Jesus' ministry moved along, He became more and more clear about how far he expected his followers to go in their pursuit of His Kingdom. Finally, Jesus revealed His ultimate sacrifice would be the death of the Cross. Nevertheless, Jesus did not reserve a Cross just for Himself. Those who would repent and come after Him are also called to take up a cross of their own. Jesus clearly taught that the only way to enter His Kingdom is to die to our whole world of dreams, plans, and associations. Every natural connection to this present world must be yielded to Jesus.

Christ's talk of His coming death on the Cross greatly upset Peter. To Peter, this seemed to be the antithesis of the way to build a kingdom. It would be the end of the movement, for how could Jesus establish His Kingdom on earth if He were to die (Matt. 16:21-23)? Peter was stuck on the man Christ Jesus and could not see past his own earthly vision of who **he thought** Jesus was. He did not see that if there was no Cross all that Jesus spoke of would be moot. Peter rebuked Jesus and told Him that this could not be the path for Him to take (v. 22). Jesus rebuked Satan who was behind the resistance to His coming work on the Cross (v. 23). I can really feel for Peter. What Jesus was proposing must have seemed so strange and upsetting. He didn't see, as we do in retrospect, that the Cross was the means that God would use to reconcile us to Himself.

While many today will accept that Jesus had to die on a Cross for our sins, that is as far as they will take it. They will accept it as a historical fact but it is to them some sort of grim and vulgar necessity. They accept it as a part of their orthodoxy of a substitutionary death and a coming resurrection. They see the Cross as a means to some day go to heaven. They are willing to go as far as **substitution** but not as far as **identification**.

Jesus clearly taught that His Cross was to be our cross by identification. Although He had to die we must also die (Matt. 16:24-25):

> *Then said Jesus unto his disciples, If any [man] will come after me, let him deny himself, and take up his cross, and follow me. For whosoever will save his life shall lose it: and whosoever will lose his life for my sake shall find it.*

Any attempt at self-preservation would nullify any claim to be His disciple. When Jesus died on the Cross all those who would follow after Him died by identification. To many this is far too extreme—it is heresy. Yet to those who will receive this truth, it becomes a pathway of life from the dead.

In John 12:24-25 Jesus stated:

> *Verily, verily, I say unto you, Except a corn of wheat fall into the ground and die, it abideth alone: but if it die, it bringeth forth much fruit. He that loveth his life shall lose it; and he that hateth his life in this world shall keep it unto life eternal.*

This is an agricultural principle. The seeming death of a seed is the only means to renew and multiply the life in the germ of the seed. Jesus was using a metaphor for His death and resurrection. He does not leave this picture at His own death. Jesus irrevocably links His death with the **death to**

self that His disciples will experience while they live their lives in this world. This is a very harsh and stark picture of repentance. Our commitment to Christ becomes a commitment to a complete denial of self, comparable to death.

Even to this day, seeds must be planted and given the appropriate conditions to grow. There is no other way than the way prescribed by nature. As with the natural, so it is with the spiritual. Jesus does not bring a patchwork quilt of human effort toward righteousness as a 'standard' for His followers. Rather, Jesus brings a stark identification with Christ in his death. We do not accept Jesus and then try to be good. We receive Jesus and forfeit our lives to Him. We gain our lives by losing our lives. A Cross-less Christianity is no Christianity at all. A repentance that doesn't take the disciple's death to self into account as a central truth is no repentance at all.

Paul the Apostle made this very clear in speaking to the Romans. Paul argued His case for living the Christian life in newness of life and victory like a lawyer argues his case—fact upon fact. He appealed to baptism as the believer's complete identification with the death and resurrection of Jesus (Romans 6:1-11). Paul appears to be answering a question posed by the church at Rome or he is answering an attitude that he had run into, related to the Cross of Christ: *"Shall we continue in sin, that grace may abound?"* (v. 1). The logic behind this question comes from a misunderstanding of Jesus' sacrifice. If Jesus died to provide a 'forgiveness vending machine' then the more we sin the more 'grace' would abound. We have clearly laid out the fact that Jesus came to save us from sin not just to forgive us in it (Matt. 1:21).

There are many today who hold to this understanding of the sacrifice of Jesus on the Cross. They assent to substitution without identification. The idea is that Jesus died for us as a substitutionary sacrifice on the Cross. Of course, this is true. Yet, without our personal identification with the death and resurrection of Christ there is no hope of really representing God's Kingdom on earth now. Our obedience could only be real at a later time when the Kingdom of God is consummated on earth.

Paul refuted this view of the Cross. He is clear that our faith in Christ's atonement has led us to a complete identification with Jesus' death. His claim is that those who have believed are *"dead to sin"* (Romans 6:2). This statement is the start of an illustration of a profound repentance. Paul's basic attitude toward sin is that it no longer should control and set the tone for the believer's life. In fact, he recommends that we reckon ourselves *"dead indeed unto sin"* (Romans 6:11). In other words, Paul is exhorting us to put the facts in evidence into action as they relate to our present life.

Paul used the believer's baptism as an illustration of his point. This was obviously his standard teaching to the Church on the meaning of baptism. The word baptism comes from the Greek word *baptizo* which speaks of a permanent immersion. A good illustration is pickles. When you cook vegetables they are dipped in the water (*bapto*) but when they are pickled they are permanently immersed in the vinegar and spices (*baptizo*). Once in the jar they no longer come in and out.

Paul uses even a more permanent illustration—death (Romans 6:3). He uses the word *"planted"*, which is exactly what happens when you die (Romans 6:5). You are buried and you walk the earth no more. This is the picture of what occurred when we received Jesus as our Savior. The old Henry died. He can no longer walk the earth. Repentance is irrevocably tied to death. We must join Jesus in the tomb (Romans 6:4) because our sinful self must be carried off to the grave. Paul's language is inclusive here—there is no alternate route to eternal life than the death of that old man of sin (Romans 6:6). The body of sin is the whole realm of sin, sins and 'The Sin', which died with Jesus on the Cross and was placed in His grave with Him. Paul is clear that this is the purpose of baptism, to illustrate what has been actually accomplished by Jesus: at its core!

Resurrection life and power inevitably follow this repentant death sentence (Romans 6:6-7). It is impossible for true Christian living to occur before we are able to identify that we died when Christ died. It is like skipping any essential step in any instruction manual! Paul's conclusion is that we must 'put it into our account' (reckon) that we are truly dead to the power and hold of sin. We are alive unto God as a result. This can never occur if the seeker does not find true repentance.

Thus the central teaching of Paul concerning the water baptism of the believer is that of full identification. For baptism to have any meaning we must have repented of our sin. This repentance acknowledges the central purpose of Christ's mission: ***"And ye know that he was manifested to take away our sins; and in him is no sin. Whosoever abideth in him sinneth not: whosoever sinneth hath not seen him, neither known him."*** (1 John 3:5-6). Here the contrast is clear. Those who have received Christ do not live in a continual life of sin; they have changed their minds and Jesus has transformed their lives so that they may walk in **liberty from sin**.

In Luke 14:26-27, Jesus illustrated death as a central key to true repentance in a very practical way:

If any man come to me, and hate not his father, and mother, and wife, and children, and brethren, and *sister, yea, and his own life also, he <u>cannot</u> be my disciple. And whosoever doth not bear his cross, and come after me <u>cannot</u> be my disciple."*

What a stark picture this gives us of the call of God. Jesus goes after the most precious associations in life. These associations include the closest family ties and the ownership of our own fate. Jesus teaches us that we must 'hate' them.

Is the bringer of love and life really coming to us with a recommendation to hate? The point is not hate, the point is **priority**. If I am willing to give God such priority that it will preempt all that is precious to me including my own self-direction then I will obviously be anxious to yield up all of my sinful behavior. All the relationships that Jesus named are legitimate associations by anybody's standards. Family is the closest and most instinctive association. There are many references in the Bible about our responsibility to provide for and live in healthy association with our family. Thus, Jesus is asserting his Lordship over all of these relationships, even the government of our own lives in the world.

Putting Christ ahead of family ties can sometimes feel a lot like dying. Jesus understood that there must be a divine Priority in life. God must rule over all worldly associations to bring them into His order and under His government. People will often use family, duty, and work as an excuse for disobeying Christ. Jesus came to give us life and there is no life without death in the Kingdom. When we put Christ's wishes ahead of the demands of family it can be very emotionally painful. Jesus said: ***"Think not that I am come to send peace on earth: I came not to send peace, but a sword... And a man's foes shall be they of his own household"*** (Matt. 10:34, 36). Family emotional ties are one of the strongest forces on the earth, yet we must be free of their pull so that Christ may reign in our hearts.

The Cross is an instrument of death. We are not called to self-denial of certain legitimate practices; we are called to denial of self which means that we are willing, at any time, to die for our King. This is repentance at its heart. We have so changed our minds about our lives that we will do anything that His rule requires. We have lost the **spiritual schizophrenia of the religious man**, separating his religion from certain areas of his life and applying his religion where he thinks it best applies. A dead person has no life at all. They will respond neither to insult or temptation. Their life is over. A resurrected man will, *"serve in newness of spirit, and not in the oldness of the letter"* (Rom. 7:6).

In response to the carnal and selfish lifestyle of the Corinthians which caused them to accuse him, Paul wrote: *"I protest by your rejoicing which I have in Christ Jesus our Lord, I die daily"* (1 Cor. 15:31). Paul was constantly exposed to the threat of death but it is clear that he is speaking of his attitude towards life. He literally *"died"* daily to his own life. Thus he experienced many deaths. In many instances and in different ways Paul refers to his identification with the death of Jesus Christ. He recommended that his followers *"reckon"* themselves dead (Rom. 6:11). Again, he spoke of his life attitude in similar terms: *"But we have this sentence of death in ourselves, that we should not trust in ourselves, but in God which raiseth the dead."* (2 Cor. 1:9). This is clearly a healthy mindset that goes with the light God sheds upon our initial repentance.

It is no new thing for the majority of people to think of the principle of death to self as too extreme and not necessary. It is clear that it is one of those matters that is *"spiritually discerned"* (1 Cor. 2:14). However, if we will allow our lives to be conformed to identify with Christ's death we will increasingly experience the new life that Jesus gives to those who live in His resurrection power. That is why 'repent' is such a beautiful word to those who believe.

What a beautiful liberty there is when we start to experience the government of God in our hearts and lives. Jesus said: ***"If the son therefore shall make you free, ye shall be free indeed"*** (John 8:36). Such freedom is not license to do as we wish but governmental power to do as He wishes. What joy comes when I identify with Jesus! It is no wonder that 'repent' is one of the most beautiful words in the vocabulary of heaven. Let us humbly ask Father to grant to us true death to our whole world of ambitions and troubles that we may enjoy the, ***"glorious liberty of the children of God"*** (Romans 8:21).

Chapter 10
The Lurking Danger

One aspect of the reign of God in each individual's life is progressive change. The process that brings the disciple toward an increasing reflection of the indwelling King is called sanctification. Jesus prayed that God would, *"Sanctify them* (His followers) *through thy truth: thy word is truth."* (John 17:17). The Greek word sanctify (*hagiazo*), comes from the root work *hagios*. This word is most often translated holy and literally means separate or away from the earth. Sanctification refers to the action of God in moving His children away from participation in the world system (*kosmos*) with its emphasis on: *"...the lust of the flesh, and the lust of the eyes, and the pride of life"* (1 John 2:16). We are sanctified when we receive Jesus and then participate in the process of sanctification for the rest of our lives.

Amazingly enough, people are not made instantly, absolutely perfect and mature by their decision to receive Christ as their Savior. When we repent there will be immediate profound change and deliverance. Nevertheless, there will be other sins and habits that will be removed and transformed by the indwelling Holy Spirit over the months and years following an individual's conversion. In fact, it is astonishing how deeply marked we are by sin. We are sinners to the core. When we believe on Christ and repent of our sin, we come into right standing with God.

In spite of this right standing, our souls have feelings that have been formed by our career of sin that reflect our former enmity with God. Our minds have thoughts and processes that exalt themselves against God. Our body has cravings and desires formed from habits that are

91

displeasing to God. The process of sanctification brings every area of the believer's life into conformity with the will of God through the power of the Holy Spirit, the Word of God, and the cleansing blood of Jesus Christ.

One of the reasons for the gradual nature of sanctification is this reality—if we saw ourselves in the fullness of our evil rebellion against God we would not be able to bear it. God, in His mercy, has a salvage aspect to the salvation that He brings to our soul. He takes the very person we are and refines us into the people He had always purposed for us to be. This comes from the moment by moment Presence of His Kingdom that dwells in our hearts. Of course, our cooperation is absolutely necessary for the Holy Spirit to do His work.

We could compare the process of sanctification with Israel's conquest of the Promised Land. Although they had been granted the Land by God, they still had to go in and conquer it. There were areas that came under their immediate control. There were areas that were harder to conquer, where they met stiff resistance and they had to believe God's promise to finally win. There were areas that they really didn't even want to conquer. Nevertheless, God had commanded them to go and conquer the whole land (Deut. 7:1ff).

The comparison between conquering the Land and the process of sanctification is useful because Paul tells us: *"Now all these things happened unto them* (Israel) *for ensamples: and they are written for our admonition, upon whom the ends of the world are come."* (1 Cor. 10:11). Paul tells us that Israel's story is a type of our story. We may learn quite a few useful lessons about the process of sanctification from the story of the conquest of the Land.

As aforementioned, all of the Land was supposed to be conquered. It was given to Israel and they were to possess it. The Books of Joshua and Judges repeat this theme many times. Nevertheless, there was pain and warfare to get the job done. They had to go forward with zeal to enjoy the benefit that was theirs. In the same way the believer is to go ahead and overcome every stronghold that will keep their life from being fruitful and reflecting the indwelling King and His Kingdom. We are to be, *"Casting down imaginations* (logical reasonings), *and every high thing that exalteth itself against the knowledge of God, and bringing into captivity every thought to the obedience of Christ."* (2 Cor. 10:5). The forts and castles of our enemy are fortresses of wrong thinking and practice in our minds and lives. We tear them down with the Word of God, the power of the Holy Spirit, and the blood of Jesus Christ.

The children of Israel were to ruthlessly drive out the nations because they were completely evil (Deut. 9:3, 4, 5; 18:12; Ezra 9:11).

> *Speak not thou in thine heart, after that the LORD thy God hath cast them out from before thee, saying, For my righteousness the LORD hath brought me in to possess this land: but for the wickedness of these nations the LORD doth Drive them out from before thee.*

The people who lived in the Land practiced child sacrifice and other abominable things. There was no peace treaty to be had because they were irrevocably evil. There was to be no association, no marriage, and no covenant with them. God's people were called to be separate.

In the same way, there is no peace treaty for the believer with their flesh, their sinful nature, or the world. We were, *"carnal, sold under sin"* (Romans 7:14). But now, *"this is the will of God, even your sanctification"* (1 Thess. 4:3). True repentance will bring about cooperation with the Holy Spirit and a participation in His program for our sanctification. As we, by the grace of God, conquer the different sins and habits that have dominated us, we grow to reflect the glory of God's reign in our hearts. Our message of salvation is backed up with the reality of a holy life. People can see Jesus in our lives and we become *"a sweet savour* (scent) *of Christ"* to everybody, both believers and unbelievers (2 Cor. 2:14-16).

It is important to note that the failure of Israel to appropriately dwell in the Land caused both a reproach and an overthrow for God's people. God allowed a series of defeats and restorations to come upon Israel because the, *"name of God is blasphemed among the Gentiles through you, even as it is written"* (Romans 2:24). We are now His people and are called by His name. It is clearly important that we do not bring reproach upon His name or His work. It is important to remember that our repentance is not to be repented of, that we must, *"continue in the faith grounded and settled, and be not moved away from the hope of the gospel"* (Col. 1:23).

We are in a sanctification process that started with a godly repentance. We do not repent every day as some people seem to think. We do go for cleansing because we still fall short of His glory. We ask for forgiveness when we sin. This is not repentance, this is cleansing; we have already repented. However, when we have a habit or sin revealed to us by the indwelling Holy Spirit, we then must repent of the sin and seek God for deliverance from it. This is the attentive day by day and moment by moment walk we have with the Lord. He keeps close accounts.

The lurking danger comes as we have been upon the way for some time and we start to think that we 'know' something. At such times, we may begin to feel that we may pick and choose what we will do for God. As well, procrastination can set in. Wherever procrastination does set in, it will hinder our obedience to God. This occurs because people tend to clear out the sins that they hate and those sins which trouble their conscience. People thus convicted are motivated for deliverance. Later, God starts to put His finger on more subtle things that we are friendlier towards. These sins usually involve what we regard as legitimate activities. Thus, repentance from such activities will mean a death to our very self-life every time.

Delayed obedience becomes sin because it violates the law of faith: ***"Therefore to him that knoweth to do good, and doeth it not, to him it is sin."*** (James 4:17). This is where the repentant and humble mind is essential. Passively regarding lethargy in our spiritual life can be deadly. Sometimes we simply don't feel like doing what God has impressed us to do. At such times we must request that God would grant us a gift of repentance. It is clear that we will not always **feel** like doing what we should and this is just where the grace of God to do His will is essential. He is able to change our mind if we will let him.

Although there is no definite scholarship to prove it, it appears that the Book of Hebrews was addressed to the Hebrew Christians in Palestine. These are the people who made huge sacrifices so that we could have the Gospel. The record of the Book of Acts is that the Hebrew believers sold what they possessed to help pay the bills for the revival in Jerusalem. They sold ancestral lands and property so that the Jewish dispersion (some of whom stayed on for years) would receive support along with those who no longer worked but preached the Gospel (Acts 2:45; 4:34-37). The result was that they became impoverished (Romans 15:25-27). These first saints sent out missionaries, including Paul, Barnabas, Mark, Silas, and the other

Apostles. They went everywhere preaching the Gospel. Eventually many of them were displaced by persecution and had to resettle elsewhere.

The occasion of the Book of Hebrews is clearer. These Hebrew people were being pressured to return to the practices of Judaism. If they were living in Palestine, they would find themselves in an impoverished situation with increasing pressure to conform to formal Jewish practice. There was no welfare state in the First Century. If you were a societal outcast with no means of support, this could bring enormous and profound financial pressure to bear. Add to this pressure a 'stepped-up' persecution and it is not hard to imagine why people would defect back to Judaism. Nevertheless, the Writer of Hebrews was clear that such compromise was sin.

In response to his exhortation to faith, the Writer of Hebrews told his audience to do two things. These seasoned Christians still needed to, *"lay aside every weight and the sin which doth so easily beset [us], and... run with patience the race that is set before us"* (Heb. 12:2). When we see sin in our heart, we must lay it aside. To continue to look at the sin and justify it, when the Holy Spirit has brought us under conviction, will bring condemnation and defeat. As well, this Christian life is a marathon, not a sprint. We must run the race with patience—it is a long race! It is much harder to run a long distance with additional weights added on. Thus, we cast away the weights! Our eye must be on the finish line, not on the immediate discomfort.

If the Hebrew Christians needed such an exhortation, how much more do we in this day? Over time, it will become clear to each believer that none of us have arrived. From time to time God will enlighten us to some new sin. Things that we may have felt justified doing in times past now come to light as evil through the revelation of God's Word. Often, the Lord will add new practices and responsibilities to our lives that require our attention. We then see that God demands a change of heart on our part.

The problem that the Hebrews were having was that they were going back and, *"...laying again the foundation of repentance from dead works,"* (Hebrews 6:1). When one of Christ's disciples goes backwards they must again repent. It is clear that this becomes hard because when we backslide we become, *"hardened through the deceitfulness of sin"* (Heb. 3:13). The lurking danger is that we will become self-deceived and start to feel that we are somehow acceptable to God in our disobedience or partial obedience.

If mature and sanctified believers like the Hebrew Christians in Palestine needed to take stock and examine whether they were still in the faith how much more do we in this day of terrible apostasy? It is clear that although we may not need to repent every day, week, or even month— from time to time we will need to repent of something that does come to light. Some people will find plenty of disobedience in their lives if they will honestly look. If we are living a lifestyle of humble dependence on God it will be easier to face, with honesty and integrity, the days when we see our need and hear the call of the Holy Spirit to repent.

The assessment and warnings given by Jesus to the Seven Churches of Revelation should be enough to make any believer sober. Many people try to spiritualize this part of the Bible to represent either succeeding stages of the historic church or to represent different types of churches that we find today. Such interpreters seem to miss the simple assessments of the Churches as given by Jesus. The cure for the evils listed is also quite simple. In every case where Jesus brought sin to light, He commanded that those in the Church involved in sin should repent. There is no mystery about Jesus' attitude.

The Churches of Ephesus, Pergamos, and Thyratira all received a long list of commendations that would satisfy many human scrutineers. These three Churches were still functioning quite well. Unfortunately, they still allowed the sins of some people to co-exist alongside those who were living righteously among the members of the Body of Christ in their town. The Ephesian Church had become so busy doing good that they had forgotten devotion to the very Jesus who died to save them (Rev. 2:4). The Church at Pegamos did not correct sexual immorality or doctrinal error in their midst (Rev. 2:14-15). The church at Thyratira wouldn't deal with a false prophetess and her doctrine of spiritual and sexual immorality (Rev. 2:20-22). Jesus' cure for their spiritual ills was that they would repent.

Two other Churches were in much worse shape. The Sardis Church had a reputation for being alive but Jesus assessed it to be dead (Rev. 3:1). The Laodicean Church had a reputation for being rich and they were spiritually impoverished (Rev. 3:17). They also were told to repent. The command to repent to all of the errant churches assumed that they **could** repent of even the most abominable backslidings. The Lord only tells us to do things that it is possible, by His grace, to do.

It is obvious that the majority of people in any of these fellowships did not have the authority to compel other people to repent. All they would have been able to do was to repent of any evil in their individual lives. The leaders had the awesome responsibility to repent themselves and then to seek to compel the rest of the believers to repent of all immorality. Jesus' solution for all of the evils of the Seven Churches was repentance. What an awesomely simple solution!

These Churches were established and appeared to prosper as far as the human eye could see. Nevertheless, Jesus was ruthless in pointing out the individual sin that would eventually cause the overthrow of many believers and the destruction of His representation in that area. He was manifested: *"to take away our sins; and in him is no sin"* (1 John 3:5). Jesus knew the power and danger of sin and He was determined that it must be repented of and cleansed away. If such stern assessment and reproof were required for First Century Churches, what scrutiny and repentance would the Lord require in our day?

Sin left unchecked in any life or fellowship produces a cumulative effect. A horse's stall needs to be cleaned thoroughly every day. You may leave it a day or two and have only minor inconvenience. Leave it for a few weeks and you have a project! Jesus seems to know that believers will sin: *"My little children, these things write I unto you, that ye sin not. And if any man sin, we have an advocate with the Father, Jesus Christ the righteous:"* (1 John 2:1). His desire is that we be clean and continue to fellowship with him.

That is why, no matter how long we have been on the way, we must cultivate a humble willingness to admit our sin and ask forgiveness; to have our minds changed by our Lord... to repent! We have come from such a sinful past that it would be foolish for us to think that we will have it all figured out after a few years. The Lord keeps working deeper into our being and when He brings new selfishness, lust, or sin to light we need to be ready, willing, and able to repent. The heart's cry of a true devotee of Jesus is: *"Search me, O God, and know my heart: try me, and know my thoughts: And see if [there be any] wicked way in me, and lead me in the way everlasting."* (Psalm 139:23-24). Let us all allow the Lord to search us. Let us repent of everything He reveals so that we may live in the true power of His resurrection.

Conclusion

Some people may ask, "What about national repentance?" They will quote 2 Chronicles 7:14ff: *"If my people, which are called by my name, shall humble themselves, and pray, and seek my face, and turn from their wicked ways..."* They will apply it to America. This ignores two important facts. Israel was the nation that received the promise. They were also the only people of God. Israel was *"the church in the wilderness"* (Acts 7:38). Therefore, the people called by His name (Israel) could repent nationally since they were the only people of God and God was the ultimate government.

Now, God's Church is made up of people from all nations who have become a *"holy nation"* to God (1 Peter 2:9). The word nation comes from the Greek *ethnos*—from which we get ethnic. Through His salvation, Jesus has created a new people who have their citizenship in heaven and represent His Kingdom as ambassadors for Christ (2 Cor. 5:10)! Thus, national repentance must first be practiced in the household of God—that is, individuals and churches but always amongst believers. Peter states it this way: *"For the time is come that judgment must begin at the house of God"* (1 Peter 4:17). God's nation is not America or any other country. There are just and unjust nations but God's nation is the Church. Therefore, it is incumbent upon all who profess to follow Jesus to apply the 'judgment' of His Word and repent wherever it is necessary.

There are many other pictures of repentance in the Bible that we may draw upon for instruction in righteousness. The picture that stands out most profoundly in my mind as a conclusion to our discussion is the picture of Jesus as He purifies the Temple. It seems apparent from Scripture that Jesus purified the Temple at the beginning and the end of His ministry. John gives us the early account and the other Gospels give us the later account. The reason given in Scripture for these purifications is because of the merchandising that was done in the place dedicated to the worship and presence of God. We can only appreciate the deeper meaning and application to our own lives as we meditate on the Temple of God, its function then, and what it pointed to prophetically.

The Temple in Jerusalem was first envisioned by King David some fifteen hundred years before Christ as a permanent dwelling place for the presence of God instead of the moveable tabernacle. David's son Solomon had the privilege of building the Temple. God Himself honored the Temple by dwelling there until the time of Jesus. It was a continuous habitation until Jesus died on the Cross and the veil was ripped in two. Then the dwelling place of God was moved from a building into the hearts and bodies of men in the Person of the Holy Spirit.

Jesus drove the money-changers and salesmen out of the Court of the Gentiles. This was the place that the non-Jew could seek Jehovah. It was sanctified to that purpose. It was part of the ministry of the Jewish people to become *"a light of the gentiles"* (Isaiah 42:6). It was God's plan that the Jewish people would reach and convert the Gentile world to the One True God. Thus, the Court of the Gentiles was a place of outreach and evangelism to the lost world. Not only were they denigrating a holy place of God with their merchandising, they were also working at cross-purposes with God. His desire was to have the whole world come to the knowledge of the truth.

At the dedication of the Temple during Solomon's reign we can see a type of the Christian life. God's presence came to abide in the Temple. This event pointed to the day when the same thing would happen within and among men—which is infinitely more useful and wonderful. Every reference to the 'Holy Temple' in the Epistles is a reference to saved human beings as the Temple, either individually, as local fellowships or as the Universal Church. Even the word 'saint' can be translated "holy one". Only God's presence through His Holy Spirit can accomplish such a work.

Jesus zealously turned Himself loose on that which defiled and degraded the Temple at Jerusalem. In the same way, when we repent, we turn Jesus loose to drive every evil and wicked thing from His present day Temple—us. What a picture this makes—Jesus with a whip in His hand, driving out every bondage and source of shame so that the Temple can become as glorious as He would have it be. No enemy would dare resist Him. When we are turned toward Jesus, there is no sin too vile or any bondage too great but that He, in His great power, can break.

So many people talk today about what they imagine is the heart of God or the heart of worship. Jesus has already told us what His heart is: *"for the son of man is come to seek and to save that which was lost"* (Luke 19:10) and *"If the Son therefore shall make you free, ye shall be free indeed"* (John 8:36). Jesus is talking about liberty from the dominion of sin. His heart is that we would repent and enjoy what he has already purchased for us on the Cross.

Let us hear and obey His invitation. Repent is the first word of the Kingdom. It is beautiful and it is simple. Even the simplest person can understand Christ's call. People have all kinds of imaginations about what God wants and what they might do for Him. He has already revealed His will: Repent! Let us not put the cart before the horse anymore but just simply take Him at His word. I know that when we really repent, our God shall abundantly pardon. Then the power of heaven will come and fill us all anew. What a glorious testimony we will become of His grace!

Appendix
A Few Helpful Hints

At the risk of repeating myself I would like to give a brief check-list for those who are truly seeking godly repentance. The most important things to remember are that our Father in Heaven is a merciful God. God is on our side. It is His great desire that we overcome sin and live a wonderful life to the praise of His glory. Here are a few helpful suggestions.

Internal Honesty & Transparency:

Ever since Adam and Eve fell, humans have been covering their sins and justifying themselves. I think it was Shakespeare that said, "To thine own self be true". I do not think Bill was an altruist. I think he was contending for internal honesty. If we fool ourselves and live in delusion we will never see the power of God turned loose on our inner man and we will never enjoy Jesus' freedom.

The key is to be honest with our Father in Heaven. He sees everything anyway. Make Him the 'audience of One' and join the Psalmist in asking: *"Search me, O God, and know my heart: try me, and know my thoughts: and see if there be any wicked way in me, and lead me in the way everlasting."* (Psalm 139:23-24). The Lord will convict us of what needs to change and He will change us for His glory.

Conviction Not Condemnation:

The Holy Spirit convicts us of sin, judgment, and righteousness. Conviction will always lead us to repent and to partake of the righteousness of God. Some people live under condemnation. They are always speaking badly of themselves and reviewing their shortcomings. Perhaps they think this is humility but it is not. God did not send Jesus to condemn the world but to save it (John 3:17). It is the devil who comes to bring condemnation by accusing us before God and to one and other.

When we are convicted by the Holy Spirit our conscience is sensitized to God's will and His Word. As we are convinced of our sin and our need, conviction moves us to call upon God. We then change our mind about sin and trust God to bring powerful positive change. We do not need to go on a witch-hunt for sin because, if our heart is soft, God will convict us about what we need to do.

Sin Lists:

It is a sure thing that we all have many blind spots. It is very much a part of human nature to be very sorry about certain sins and to be very comfortable with others. God, in His wisdom, has several lists of sins or 'works of the flesh' recorded that we need to look at prayerfully and say, "Is this me?" Although these lists are not meant to be exhaustive, they cover many areas and tendencies. They are like a list of the symptoms of the activity of an underlying disease. Some of the words used for certain sins are worth studying out for their deeper meaning in the original language.

Some of the sin lists are: Mark 7:17-23; Romans 1:19-23, 3:10-18; Gal. 5: 19-21; Col. 3:5-10; Eph. 4: 22-31. There is either a hint or a solution that comes with each list. Jesus teaches us that wicked deeds come from an internal struggle. If we will repent, this will resolve the internal struggle (although we will still be tempted from without). In Romans, Paul lists sins to prove that we all are sinners but he is arguing a greater point—that the *"law of the spirit of life"* can bring us victory over all sin (Romans 8:2). When the other lists exhort us to 'put off' or 'mortify' the deeds of the flesh we then see that it is to be clothed with Christ's character.

Fill The House:

Jesus gave us an unusual insight into the spirit-world in Luke 11:14-26. He taught that when an evil spirit was driven away from a person that it suffered in a desert-like atmosphere. The spirit would assuredly go back and check how his old house was doing. If the delivered person had not filled the house it gave the unclean spirit an opportunity to come back. There is a greater lesson here for us.

Jesus taught that it was not sufficient to empty our lives of evil behavior. When we have been sinning we have been filling our 'house' with evil behavior. When we quit sinning it is imperative that we fill the empty spaces with the goodness of God. We are not just given lists of 'don'ts' but also 'do's'. Thus, repentance has as much to do with walking out God's righteousness as it does with putting off evil behavior. We are given many lists of what constitutes 'fruit' in the Christian life. Some of these lists are Gal. 5:22-25; Eph. 4:22-29, 32; 5:8-10; 1 Cor. 13; Col. 3: 10-25. The person who is seeking to do good deeds has difficulty finding the time for evil.

Confess To Another Human Being:

James 5:26 tells us: *"confess your faults one to another, and pray one for another, that ye may be healed. The effectual fervent prayer of a righteous man availeth much."* Most of us have done things that we don't want everyone to know about. Nevertheless, there are times when it is very useful to confess to another **reliable** person who will keep our confidence. When we come clean, the devil finds it harder to accuse us and we find relief. There is something liberating in repenting before another person. Sometimes it is really appropriate to repent before many people. It is humbling but when we humble ourselves, God draws near. The promise is that we will be healed. Another benefit of confession is that it is wonderful to have those to whom we have confessed effectively praying for us. People cannot pray for you unless they know the real needs you have. This gives them an opportunity to show their love for us.

Renounce, Resist, Persist:

It is very useful to verbally **renounce** that which we are repenting of. We may confess that we have **loved** the behavior in the past but we are now choosing to hate and forsake it. Almost every time we repent of something new, we will be tempted to do it again. We have the promise of God that if we **resist** the devil he will flee from us (James 4:7). We then must **persist**. Perseverance is a characteristic of those who overcome the devil. Those who persevere are called 'overcomers' (Rev. 12:11): *"And they overcame him* (the devil) *by the blood of the Lamb, and by the word of their testimony; and the loved not their lives unto the death."* You can only be an 'overcomer' if you overcome something. We must hold our ground and not let emotional swings sway us back and forth from good to evil.

Quit Judging Others:

To see astonishing success, quit judging, talking about, and condemning others. Again, James 2:12-13 tells us: *"So speak ye, and so do, as they that shall be judged by the law of liberty. For he shall have judgment without mercy, that hath shewed no mercy, and mercy rejoiceth against judgment."* Weighing this with other Scriptures on the subject, it seems that I will determine the severity of my own judgment by the standards that I impose upon others. As well, I have learned that I bring trials and temptations upon myself when I start judging others. Somehow, God is so faithful that He will readily point out our own weakness and hypocrisy when we sit as judges over others. How liberating it is to realize that we only have to give an account for ourselves.

Reconciliation & Restitution:

Many people try to function in God's Kingdom when they have not dealt with their human relationships. There are many Scriptures that speak about forgiveness. We must forgive others. As well, we have wronged others. Many people could receive profound and immediate healing if they went to the people they had wronged in the past and asked their forgiveness. This may seem like hard medicine but if we truly repent it includes repenting to those we have wronged. **Reconciliation** will often bring surprising opportunities for testimony and even joyful restoration of seemingly unfixable rifts.

Sometimes we have stolen, failed to pay debts, committed crimes, or just done other people wrong. At such times it is appropriate to make **restitution**. This can be very expensive but if I have truly repented of sin it is the only reasonable response. So many people are held in bondage because they have not brought forth *"fruits worthy of repentance"* (Luke 3:8). Again, when we make restitution, we will often be astonished at the joy we feel, the testimony that comes, and the release we receive from our sin.

<u>Deliverance</u>:

Often, sin in our life will invite the activity of demons. An individual who has lived a persistently evil life has given the devil grounds to lay stronger and stronger hold upon them. Most often, if we will follow the above steps with holy determination, we will identify and run off demonic activity in our lives. Sometimes our repentance will reveal a profound underlying bondage from Satan. At such times it is wise to find other believers to assist in receiving deliverance from the devil.

This is no job for a novice or those who don't believe in deliverance. In some quarters there are those who profess to have such a ministry but have little success when it comes time to get the job done. Those who will have success are easy to identify. Firstly, they have deeply and profoundly repented themselves. They are clean and holy and reflect the light of Jesus. Those who participate in such ministry need to be mature Christians who know their authority. They will be full of the Holy Spirit, which is the Finger of God to drive out demons. It is amazing how the LORD will bring such persons across our path when we need them.

Faith:

Finally, Jesus told us to *"have faith in God"* (Mark 11:22). That is better translated *"have the faith of God"*. God wishes to impart His faith to our heart. We can be assured that He will bring us through to victory every time. We must come to every circumstance of repentance with a mind full of faith toward God. If we nurture a life of faith we will assuredly please God for the Scripture saith: *"The just shall live by faith"* (Hab. 2:4; Rom. 1:17; Gal. 3:11; Heb. 10:38). Our success does not depend on us but upon Him. Our Father cannot lie or fail, so let us submit to Him as His workmanship.

A Prayer Of Repentance Unto Salvation

Most holy God, my Father.
I come to You in the name of Jesus Your Son.
I confess now that I have sinned
many sins against you.
I am a sinner.
I believe that Jesus died as a
sacrifice for my sin.
I am truly sorry for my sin.
I repent of my sin and ask You, Father,
to grant me a repentant mind and heart.
Forgive my sins.
Jesus, come into my heart and be my Savior.
I receive you as the LORD, the Boss of my life.
Come and reign in my life.
I love you God.
I will serve you for the rest of my life,
but only by Your grace and power.
Thank You Father.
I believe Your Word which tells me:
If I confess my sins, You are faithful
And just to forgive my sins,
And to cleanse me from all unrighteousness!
In Jesus' Name, Amen!